Bratis

THE BRADT CITY

Lucy Mallows

Bradt Travel Guides Ltd, UK
The Globe Pequot Press Inc, USA

First published December 2005

Bradt Travel Guides Ltd
23 High Street, Chalfont St Peter, Bucks SL9 9QE, England; www.bradtguides.com
Published in the USA by The Globe Pequot Press Inc, 246 Goose Lane, PO Box 480,
Guilford, Connecticut 06437-0480

A catalogue record for this book is available from the British Library

ISBN-10: 1 84162 142 0   ISBN-13: 978 1 84162 142 5

Front cover City square with street cafés, fountain and clock tower (Reinhard Schmid/Fototeca 9x12)
Text photographs John Burke (JB), Andrea Anca-Strauss (AAS)
Maps Steve Munns. Based on maps supplied by Mapa Slovakia   *Illustrations* Carole Vincer

Typeset from the author's disc by Wakewing
Printed and bound in Spain by Grafo SA, Bilbao

Author

Born and educated in the UK, **Lucy Mallows** spent 12 years in Budapest working as a writer and editor. Recently she moved to Brussels where she works as a freelance travel writer and translator. She contributes regularly to many international dailies and magazines and has written for all the top travel publishers on countries from Estonia to Portugal. She is an expert on central Europe and speaks six foreign languages, including Russian and Hungarian. Her passions are travel, soul music and Chelsea FC.

DEDICATION

To my dear late dad, who always insisted he first sent me 'out east'; to my mum who was relieved it wasn't Ulan Bator; and to Ágnes Szarka who still hasn't recovered from our day trip to Kunszentmiklós.

Contents

Contents

Acknowledgements

To Saša Bučková and her team at BKIS, ever ready with help and ideas.

To Milan Vajda at the Mayor's office for his time and insights.

To Lenka Šoltysová, Tomas Ondrčka, Karin Laliková, Igor Baďura and Štefan Ďurajka for making my visit comfortable.

To Tom Nicholson for an insider's yet fresh 'spectator's' view of the city.

To Andreea Anca-Strauss for photographic creativity.

To Mrs Romankevich, my Russian teacher at Bishop Fox's Grammar School, who inspired in me a love and fascination for all things Slavic and set me off on a long, 25-year journey which finally reached its destination: Bratislava!

Thanks to Adrian Phillips for thinking of me for this project and keeping my brain sharp with Hungarian-language questions during my Slavic sojourn.

To Hilary Bradt, Tricia Hayne, Selena Dickson, Debbie Everson, Kate Lyons, Anna Moores, Janet Mears and everyone else at Bradt who helped make *Bratislava* such an enjoyable and smooth-running experience.

FEEDBACK REQUEST

Bratislava is constantly evolving, changing and improving.

I've tottered the length and breadth of the city and its environs, scribbling notes about those museums, shops, cafés, bars, restaurants, parks, churches and even cemeteries that I hope will be of use to those who want to know Bratislava better.

However, I'm sure there was a back street I missed or a café that has opened since my last visit. Please let me know and I'll endeavour to update the next edition and achieve an even more comprehensive version.

I look forward to reading your tips, ideas, personal reflections, criticism (constructive, hopefully!) by email at bratislavaguide@yahoo.co.uk or by snail mail c/o Bradt Travel Guides, 23 High Street, Chalfont St Peter, Bucks SL9 9QE.

Na zdravie! (Cheers!) Lucy

Introduction

I first visited Bratislava in spring 1982, while studying at Brno University near by. In the pre-Velvet Revolution, pre-Velvet Divorce days, Bratislava was a charming, if sleepy, provincial town in Czechoslovakia and I stayed with a hospitable Slovak family in what I now realise was a very swanky apartment on a street leading up to the castle.

Ironically, given all my Slavic studies, my fate became intertwined with Hungary from 1986 onwards and I lived in Budapest for 12 years; however, I frequently visited Bratislava to practise my Slovak verbs (over several litres of Slovak beer) and observe its evolution from sleepy and quiet to cosmopolitan and go-getting.

I can't help but compare and contrast with Budapest, having lived there so long, yet Bratislava comes off extremely well against its more famous big brother.

Bratislava's small size is satisfying. You have the sense that you can discover everything in a few days, see all the important sights and get a real feel for the place without the nagging, lingering doubt that you might have missed something secret or spectacular. In spring, the Old Town turns into one giant outdoor café; it has a very Mediterranean feel with endless eating and drinking possibilities and superb quality at extremely reasonable prices. Slovak people are not grim Eastern Bloc types, but instead are unusually relaxed for a country that has seen so much tragedy and trauma.

I mustn't forget the Opera House. I was spoilt for cultural choice in Budapest but I reckon Bratislava's opera rivals those in Budapest and Vienna and the ticket prices are astounding – €2 for a last-minute ticket is mind-blowing.

Bratislava is also very green. There are many places to sit back and relax in the sunshine, or for the more energetic, endless opportunities for sports such as hiking, canoeing and cycling. Why not combine exercise with another of Slovakia's natural attributes and sample the excellent wines along the Small Carpathian Wine Route? And have I mentioned the world-beating beer at jaw-dropping prices yet?

So, congratulations for stepping off the beaten path and trying out Bratislava. Your pioneering spirit will pay dividends; think of all the money you'll save on the beer and be sure to tell all your friends about your discovery. Or maybe not; let's keep this our special, Slovak secret.

Bratislava, the 'little big city' is modest, charming and pocket-sized, like its cathedral. It doesn't bellow its beauty like Prague but states its case quietly and insistently, until suddenly you wake up one gorgeous Slovak spring morning and realise you're in love.

How to use this book

Symbols are used where appropriate to indicate transport routes: $\overline{\text{B}}$ bus; $\overline{\text{T}}$ tram; $\overline{\text{TB}}$ trolleybus; $\overline{\text{NB}}$ nightbus.

Map references (eg: [1 C4] in *Chapters 5, 6* and *10*) relate to the colour maps at the end of this guide.

Hotels are divided by price range (not by area), in the Slovak style of stars, from luxurious to one-star (basic).

Restaurants are divided by area – Old Town and Castle District, and Centrum and further afield. Prices were verified within four months and will only have gone up by a few koruna, but please use them as a comparative guide.

Opening hours are included for restaurants, bars, museums and sights.

Chapter 9 (*Walking tours*) includes cross references to *Chapter 10* (*Museums and sightseeing*) and also *Chapter 6* (*Eating and drinking*).

Time is given in local Slovak style, using the 24-hour clock.

Money/prices are given in Slovak koruna (Sk) and/or their euro equivalent at the time of going to press. Many hotels and some shops and restaurants now accept euros. Many also take credit cards (indicated in the listings).

Pocket an expert!
More city guides from Bradt

Comprehensive coverage of a range of European cities,
complemented by full-colour street maps.

Belgrade Laurence Mitchell

From walking tours of the Serbian capital and tips on the best shopping and café pit-stops to essential words and phrases to help you order the local specialities, *Belgrade* contains all the information needed to enjoy what this increasingly popular city has to offer

Budapest Adrian Phillips & Jo Scotchmer

This guide offers a fascinating insight into one of the world's great romantic capitals. A wide range of options are covered – including the caves and Roman ruins of Buda, the vibrant shops and restaurants of Pest, and the city's best walks and thermal spas.

Dubrovnik Piers Letcher

Piers Letcher brings his in-depth knowledge of Croatia to this historic walled town, fast becoming a popular short-break destination. Here is everything for that idyllic break, from nightlife and the best local restaurants to island retreats and nearby national parks.

Ljubljana Robin & Jenny McKelvie

Slovenia's capital blends Austro-Hungarian and Italian influences, offering a lively nightlife buzz and classic cultural attractions. Travellers are provided with a range of places to stay, from new luxury hotels to family-run guesthouses that retain their typical Slovenian charm.

Available from all good bookshops, or by post, phone or internet direct from:

Bradt Travel Guides Ltd

Tel: +44 (0)1753 893444 www.bradtguides.com

BRATISLAVA AT A GLANCE

Location In the southwestern corner of Slovakia, where it borders Austria and Hungary. Only 60km from Vienna, the two cities are the closest capitals in the world. The state border with Hungary is just 16km away, in fact just beyond Bratislava city limits.

Climate Warm, wet summers; cold, cloudy, humid winters.

Population 451,616

Languages/official language Slovak (official), Hungarian

Religion Roman Catholic 68.9%, Evangelical Church of the Augsburg Confession 6.9%, Greek-Catholic 4.1%, Reformed Christian 2%, Orthodox 0.9%, Jehovah's Witness 0.4%, Evangelic Methodist 0.1%, Brethren Baptist Union 0.1%, Without religious affiliation 16.6%

Currency Slovak koruna (Slovenská koruna): 1 Slovak koruna (Sk) = 100 halier (h); bank notes with a value of 20, 50, 100, 200, 500, 1,000, 5,000Sk, coins with a value of 1, 2, 5, 10Sk

Exchange rate £1 = 57Sk, US$1 = 32Sk, €1 = 39Sk (October 2005)

International dialling code Slovakia: +421, Bratislava: 02

Time CET (GMT + 1 hour)

Electrical voltage 220 volts, frequency 50Hz; two-pin plugs

Contents

'The only thing I know about Slovakia is what I learned first-hand from your foreign minister who came to Texas,' George W Bush told a Slovak journalist, shortly after meeting the prime minister of Slovenia. Slovakia, it seems, still has a lot of PR work to do.

However, the legendary Casanova knew Bratislava and he knew a thing or two about beauty. He declared it 'the most beautiful city in Europe'. Bratislava is a good-looking town filled with good-looking people, who look like they're enjoying life.

Because the city has been conquered so many times, the gene pool has been shaken up, resulting in a handsome population, especially the women. The economy is thriving and many low-cost airlines now fly direct to Bratislava, bringing in not only stag parties to appreciate the beer and the ladies, but businessmen and women eager to do business in the most vibrant economy in the region.

You would never guess from walking around Bratislava's peaceful, gentle, spruced-up Old Town centre with its pedestrian heart and almost Mediterranean terrace-café culture, but the city's history is more turbulent and traumatised than that of most other countries in the region. What other city in Europe has been capital of two vastly different nations and cultures?

Bratislava sits right at the strategic meeting point of three countries – Slovakia, Austria and Hungary – and played a vital and deeply significant role in the mighty Habsburg Empire.

The city was also the capital of Hungary for more than 300 years while Slovakia was part of Hungary for the best part of a millennium.

Bratislava's Old Town was completely refurbished, buffed up and cleaned in 1999 and has never looked so good. However, Bratislava definitely suffers from an identity crisis. It's not exactly an inferiority complex, although it would be forgiven for having one after all the unkind comments. Visiting Hungarians say either 'Oh, we used to own all this' or 'It's just like a small Hungarian country town'. Visiting Czechs say 'It's not the new Prague', but Bratislava is not Prague, and it's probably quite happy being itself.

Bratislava has also been called a 'suburb' of Vienna as it sits right at the far western end of Slovakia. Look at the map and Bratislava is much nearer to Vienna (obviously), Budapest, Prague, Zagreb and Salzburg than to most of its own eastern Slovakian cities: Kosice and certainly Medzilaborce in the far east of the country, home of Andy Warhol's parents.

To the endless irritation of the two countries, Slovakia is always getting confused with Slovenia. The February 2005 summit between presidents Vladimir Putin and George W Bush was supposed to put Slovakia firmly on the map, right in the heart of Europe as an important member of the EU. However, the maps were just the start of the problem. CNN produced a series of 'helpful' maps, most of which missed off Slovakia entirely, marking just the Czech Republic or incorporating it into a Magyar irredentist's dream of 'greater Hungary'. *USA Today* went one further and placed Slovakia down by the Adriatic, between Italy and

INTERESTING TRIVIA

1 Bratislava is the new Europe's newest capital city (1993).

2 Bratislava and Vienna are the closest capitals in the world (only 64km apart).

3 Bratislava has been the capital of two very different countries (Hungary and Slovakia).

4 The post office on Námestie Slobody is the largest in the world, although nowadays, the building is mostly occupied by the Ministry of Telecommunications.

5 The town's Nový most (New Bridge) was completed in 1972 as the finishing touch to a communist highway running smack bang through the centre of the city. The project required the destruction of 226 buildings in Bratislava's Old Town. During the 20th century, two-thirds of the Old Town was destroyed, which is perhaps why the district feels so small and cosy today.

Croatia, in Slovenia's position, and the only benefit was that it got a seaside.

Slovaks and Slovenes are equally irritated by the inability of foreigners, even some Europeans, to distinguish the vastly differing countries, 440km and five hours' drive apart (and that's bombing down the motorway). It probably doesn't help matters

Contexts

that the Slovak word for Slovakia is Slovensko, which sounds a bit like…oh dear.

Bratislava, the new Europe's newest capital, has been enjoying its EU status for 18 months now and has embraced a Westward-looking mentality with a new-found self confidence.

Slovakia has made the transition with more ease than most other central European countries and that ease is symbolised by its capital Bratislava, a city that always was at the strategic heart of events and which has now found its rightful place in the new Europe.

HISTORY
The early years

Archaeological finds have shown the existence of man in the area now known as Slovakia from the middle Palaeolithic era (200000–35000BC). The region where Bratislava now stands was colonised in the 5th millennium BC and Slovakia was a significant centre for bronze production. The **Celtic tribes** settled here in the 5th century BC and four centuries later, the **Celts** built fortified settlements on the Danube banks at Bratislava and Devín nearby. The strategic advantages were developed in AD400 when **Gerulata** became a Roman staging post. Remnants of this can still be seen at Rusovce, 5km downriver from central Bratislava.

Slavic tribes arrived in the region during the 5th century and the empire of **Samo**, a Frankish warrior merchant, was established two centuries later.

Great Moravian Empire

Christianity came with the establishment of the **Great Moravian Empire** in AD833. This empire encompassed the lands of modern Slovakia and Moravia as well as parts of Hungary, Austria, Bohemia and the southern part of Poland. In AD828, during the reign of **Prince Pribina**, the first Christian church in central Europe was built in Nitra, the ancient home of Slovak princes.

In AD863, at the invitation of Great Moravian Prince Rastislav, the brothers and missionaries **Cyril and Methodius** came from Thessaloniki to Great Moravia and created the Old Church Slavonic alphabet, the origins of today's **Cyrillic** alphabet. They also translated liturgical books into Old Church Slavonic, which they codified.

The Middle Ages and the Magyars

In AD907, after much political intrigue, the Great Moravian Empire collapsed and the region was invaded by the Magyars whose King St István (Stephen) founded the **Christian Hungarian State** in the Carpathian Basin in 1000. By the end of the 11th century, Slovakia had become an integral and the most developed part of old Hungary, a relationship which was to last for almost 1,000 years, despite rude interruptions by the Tartars in 1241, the Turks in 1526 and the Habsburgs for more than 300 years.

The territory now known as the Slovak Republic was then called **Felvidék** ('Upper Countryside' in Hungarian) and remained so until the end of World War I.

Between the 11th and 15th centuries, the region experienced a period of great economic growth and cultural advancement. In 1291, **King András III** granted Bratislava the privileges of a royal free town and in 1436 **King Sigismund of Luxembourg** granted the city a coat of arms featuring a castle. During the Renaissance, and particularly the enlightened rule of **King Mátyás Corvinus**, cultural life blossomed in Bratislava. The **Academia Istropolina**, the first university in what is now Slovakia, was founded.

Ottomans and Habsburgs

Life in the entire region was to change dramatically in 1526 at the **Battle of Mohács** (in southern Hungary), when the Ottoman forces wiped out the Hungarian army on one tragic day. The Habsburgs assumed the Hungarian crown and ten years later, after the fall of Buda, when the Turks had taken the city, the **capital of Hungary** was moved to Bratislava (Pozsony in Hungarian, Pressburg in German). Many of the following conflicts, when Hungarian nobles sided with Turks in continuous efforts to dislodge the Habsburgs, were played out on the territory of Slovakia.

In 1536, Pressburg became not only the capital of Hungary, but also the centre of all administrative offices and the seat of the Hungarian archbishop. The Hungarian crown jewels were moved to Pressburg in 1552 and between 1563 and 1830 a total of 19 Hungarian kings and queens were crowned in **St Martin's Cathedral**. In 1683, with the help of the Polish king, **Ján Sobieski**, the Habsburgs defeated the Turks who had almost reached the gates of Vienna. The Turks were driven out of central Europe for good.

Maria Theresa was crowned in St Martin's Cathedral in 1741 and towards the end of the 18th century, her reforms and those of her son Joseph II formed the basis of a modern state administration, tax and transportation system, army and schools and made life a little easier for Slovaks.

Bratislava's time of prominence came to an end in 1783 when the capital returned to Buda. However, coronations were held in the city until 1830 and the Magyar presence still affected all aspects of life.

The Slovak National Awakening (národné obrodenie)

By the late 18th century, the Slovaks were attempting to assert their national and cultural identity and rise up against Hungarian domination, similar to their neighbouring Czechs' reaction against German overlords. In 1792, the linguist **Anton Bernolák** founded the Slovak Learned Society (Slovenské učené tovarišstvo) in Modra, near Bratislava. He was joined by many Slovak intellectuals who recognised the opportunity of subverting the Austro-Hungarian monarchy. The lower classes were not inspired until 1843, when **Ľudovít Štúr**, the son of a Lutheran pastor, codified the Slovak literary language. Previously all literature was written in Czech. This made the Slovak nationalist movement more accessible to ordinary Slovaks.

By 1848, **revolutions** were widespread in Europe. The Hungarian uprising against the Habsburgs was inspired by the poet Sándor Petôfi, born in Kiskőrös,

Hungary, but with Slovak roots (his name registered at his first school in Aszód, Hungary, was Alexander Petrovič). Slovakia was desperate for change and volunteer groups formed in many parts of the country to battle against the Habsburgs.

The **Slovak National Council** (Slovenská národná strana) developed as the first representative Slovak political organ of modern history. In 1849 its members endeavoured, through co-operation with Vienna, to effect the separation of Slovakia from Hungary and its incorporation as an autonomous entity within the system of the federal Habsburg monarchy. In 1861, the **Martin Memorandum** issued in the town of Martin in central Slovakia, urged the establishment of a Slovak district and language within Greater Hungary and two years later saw the foundation of a cultural and educational foundation, **Matica Slovenská** (Little Mother of the Slovaks). This was an important moment for the Slovaks as it confronted the Hungarian oppressors head-on.

In 1867, the Austrian Empire, after suffering humiliating defeats against Prussia and Italy, was forced to sign a **Compromise** (*Ausgleich* in German or *Kiegyezés* in Hungarian) with Hungary and create a dual monarchy. For the Slovaks this was nothing short of disaster. Slovakia was still 'Felvidék' (Upper Countryside) and the Slovaks were subjected to an even more ruthless programme of 'Magyarisation'. This policy made Hungarian the only language in schools and large swathes of land were confiscated for use by Hungarian settlers, causing hardship throughout the country. By the outbreak of World War I, almost 20% of Slovaks had emigrated, mostly to the USA.

Contexts

World War I

When war broke out, the Slovaks and Czechs decided that they would be better off together, uniting with their Slavic brothers, the Serbs and Russians and large numbers defected from the Austro-Hungarian armies to fight against them on the Eastern Front.

In 1915, representatives of the Slovak and Czech ethnic organisations went to the USA to sign the **Cleveland Agreement**, brokered by President Woodrow Wilson, which established a common federal state. Under the **Pittsburgh Agreement**, the autonomous position of Slovakia within a democratic Czechoslovak Republic was proclaimed.

By the end of World War I, the notion of establishing an independent Czecho-Slovakia was fully supported by the United States, England, France and Italy. On 28 October 1918, the **Czecho-Slovak National Committee** in Prague proclaimed the existence of Czecho-Slovakia. Two days later, in the **Martin Declaration**, the Slovak National Council declared its desire for Slovakia to join with the Czech lands in one common state.

On 1 January 1919, Pressburg (in German, Pozsony in Hungarian) was occupied by Czechoslovak legions and annexed to the new Czechoslovak Republic. The city's name was changed to **Bratislava**, which had a more Slavic sound and suggested the glory (*sláva*) of Slavic brother (*brat*) hood, while also referring to earlier names of the city. The skilful politician **Tomáš Masaryk** became president of the new republic from 1918 to 1935 and did much to defend democracy.

history

On 5 June 1920, the **Treaty of Trianon** returned the territory of Slovakia to the Slovaks and confirmed the controversial new border with Hungary along the Danube River. However, this carving up of central Europe left some 750,000 Hungarians stranded on Slovak soil.

World War II

The **new republic** of Czechoslovakia inherited 80% of the Austro-Hungarian industry in the region but also a diverse and tricky blend of peoples in its population.

In the 1930s, as the world plunged into Depression, Czechoslovakia began to crumble under internal tensions. The 1935 elections saw victory for the Hlinka Party, the Agrarian Party and the Hungarian Agrarian Party.

Masaryk died in 1937, leaving the less capable socialist deputy, **Edvard Beneš** in charge of the Czech lands, part of which, the mainly German-speaking Sudetenland region, had been annexed by Hitler. Hitler summoned the Slovak People's Party leader, **Jozef Tiso**, a Catholic priest and staunch nationalist, to Munich and gave him an ultimatum: either declare independence as a **Nazi puppet state** or we will carve up Slovakia between Germany, Hungary and Poland. On 14 March 1939, the Slovak parliament voted unanimously for independence. Beneš resigned on 5 October 1939 and German troops took the Sudetenland and the rest of the Czech region.

Wartime Slovakia's 'independence' lasted from 1939 to 1945, during which time Tiso banned all opposition parties, instituted censorship along Nazi lines and deported Jews to the **extermination camps** of Sobibor, Majdanka, Treblinka and

Auschwitz-Birkenau. **Deportation** began in March 1942 and in seven months, 74,000 had been taken away. **Tiso** was very anti-Semitic and he terrorised the people with the fascist Hlinka Guard whose symbol was a sinister double cross. Recently, it was revealed that Tiso struck a deal with the Nazis and paid them 500 Reichsmarks for each Jew taken away. The Nazis promised 'they will never come back'. Tiso fled the country in 1945 and was captured, tried and executed. To this day, Tiso remains a highly controversial figure in Slovak history. A play now showing at Bratislava's **Aréna Theatre** examines the character, and also, more worryingly, on the anniversary of the 14 March 1939 declaration of Slovak independence, skinheads make a habit of gathering at Tiso's grave in Martinský cemetery. However, not all Slovaks supported the puppet Nazi state and in August 1944, the **Slovak National Uprising** (Slovenské národné povstanie, or **SNP**) took place. It was quashed within two months by German troops, at Tiso's request, but the SNP is still remembered in street, bridge and square names throughout the country.

Post-war and communism

In April 1945, Czechoslovakia was 'liberated' by the **Red Army**. At this time, the Slovak state collapsed and Czecho-Slovakia was once again united, this time as a centralised state based in Prague.

In 1948, an ailing President Beneš resigned and died shortly afterwards. His place was taken by former Communist Party leader **Klement Gottwald**. A programme of Stalinisation began with five-year plans, arrests, class war and gulags.

The Prague Spring

On 5 January 1968, the Stalinist First Secretary Antonín Novotný was replaced by a young Slovak reformist **Alexander Dubček**. He encouraged civil society and freedom of expression in what was called 'socialism with a human face'. Dubček implemented the 1960 constitution granting Czechs and Slovaks equal rights as separate yet federal states and the optimistic period of 1968 became known as the **Prague Spring**.

On 21 August 1968, the Soviet tanks, supported by Warsaw Pact troops, rolled into Prague, Bratislava and other towns and wiped out all of Dubček's reforms. The Czech and Slovak republics remained separate in name, but the real power stayed in Prague.

Velvet Revolution, Velvet Divorce

In November 1989, the fall of the **Iron Curtain** enabled the establishment of a democratic government, the restoration of civil freedom and human rights. On 24 November, Dubček appeared on a balcony above Wenceslas Square in Prague alongside former playwright turned Charter 77 spokesperson, **Vaclav Havel**. On 27 November, a general strike was held throughout the country and the people of Bratislava also demonstrated in the streets supporting student movements and the Public against Violence and Civic Forum initiatives. The bloodless demonstrations were later dubbed the **Velvet Revolution**.

After the Velvet Revolution, Slovaks were keen for autonomy and in February 1992 rejected a treaty that would have continued with a federal Czechoslovakia.

The Czechs and Slovaks could not even agree on whether or not there should be an official hyphen in the name between Czecho and Slovakia.

Independent Slovakia

In June 1992, the left-leaning government of **HZDS** (Hnutie za Demokratické Slovensko or Movement for a Democratic Slovakia) was elected, headed by the populist leader **Vladimír Mečiar**, a staunch supporter of Slovak independence. Pushed on by Mečiar, the Slovak parliament proclaimed the sovereignty of the Slovak Republic in July 1992 and the Slovak Constitution was signed on 3 September 1992.

On 1 January 1993 Slovakia celebrated the **Velvet Divorce**, when the newly independent and sovereign Slovak Republic came into being, followed six weeks later by the election of the first democratic Slovak president, **Michal Kováč**, once an HZDS ally of Mečiar, but now less of a friend.

Slovakia gained **independence** in 1993 and for the first years it lurked in the shadow of the populist authoritarian rule of Vladimír Mečiar, a former boxer and inflammatory public speaker. Slovakia became a member of the UN, OSCE, IMF etc but the internal politics and economy got into a severe crisis. Compared with 1989, in 1993 the GDP dropped to 74%, and previously unknown mass unemployment appeared. Slovak industry, producing until then mainly for the Soviet market, collapsed. Foreign investors also hesitated because of the uncertain political climate. Mečiar carried out a relentless campaign to remove Kováč from office, and rumours abound that he was behind the bizarre kidnapping in August 1995 of Kováč's son Michal, who was blindfolded, given electric shocks to his genitals, forced to drink a bottle of whisky and then abandoned in a car boot in Vienna.

Dates in the history of Bratislava and Slovakia

Walking around Bratislava's beautiful, peaceful Old Town centre, it's hard to guess its turbulent and busy history, never mind all the different names it has been called. Here is a brief summary of the events which took place within the elegant walls, and for simplicity's sake, the city is always referred to as Bratislava. To check out the ever-changing names see box *Town identity* (pages 16–17).

5000BC	Colonisation of Bratislava in the late Stone Age
500BC	Illyrians settle in the region now known as Slovakia
100BC	Celts build fortified settlements at Devín and Bratislava and establish a mint producing silver coins called 'Biatecs'
AD400	Gerulata – Roman staging post, today called Rusovce, near Bratislava
AD500	Slavic tribes arrive in the region now known as Slovakia
AD830–906	Great Moravian Empire
AD864	Dowina – the first written reference to Devín Castle in the *Fulda Almanacs*
AD907	Braslavespurch – the first written reference to Bratislava in the *Salzburg Almanacs*

AD1000	King St Stephen founds the Christian Hungarian state
1018–1918	Slovakia under Hungarian rule (with brief periods of uprising)
1241	Slovakia invaded by Tartars (1241–42 Tartars plunder Hungary)
1291	The privilege of the royal free town, granted by King András III
1436	King Zsigmond grants a coat of arms to Bratislava (featuring a castle)
1465	Academia Istropolitana – first university in what is now Slovak territory founded by King Mátyás Corvinus
1526	Battle of Mohács (southern Hungary, Ottoman Turks invade the country) and Habsburgs assume the Hungarian crown
1536	The fall of Buda, Ottomans take over Buda, Hungarian capital moves to Bratislava
	First session of the Hungarian Parliament in Bratislava (last session in 1848)
1536–1783	Bratislava is made capital of Hungary. It remains the capital of Hungary, the assembly town and seat of the central administrative offices until 1783 when the capital returns to Buda.
1543	Bratislava becomes the seat of the Hungarian Archbishop
1552–1783	The Hungarian royal crown jewels are kept in the Bratislava Crown Tower, then moved to Vienna
1563–1830	Bratislava is the Coronation town for 19 Hungarian kings and queens
1683	Habsburgs defeat Turks almost at gates of Vienna

1711	Plague epidemic during which 3,860 people die
1741	Coronation of Maria Theresa in St Martin's Cathedral in Bratislava
1775	Queen Maria Theresa orders city walls to be pulled down; further development of the city
1776	Establishment of the Theatre of Estates with a permanent company of actors

TOWN IDENTITY

Reflecting the turbulent history and different succession of occupants and occupiers, the city's name has also varied over the centuries. In the Old Town Hall, they have collected all the names:

AD805	Wratislaburgum
AD907	Braslavespurch
1038	Breslava Civitas
1042	Brezezburg
1050	Brezalauspurch
1052	Preslawaspurch
1108	Bresburg, Bresburch
1146	Bosonium

Contexts

1780	Establishment of first manufacturer in Bratislava
1783	Capital of Hungary moves back to Buda
1792	Anton Bernolák founds the Slovak Learned Society in Modra, part of a national cultural awakening in Slovakia
1805	The signing of the Pressburg Peace Treaty in the Primate's Palace after battle of three emperors at Austerlitz

1300s–1400s	Poson, Posonium
1465	Istropolis
1500s	Posonium Pressburg
1848	Pozsony Pressburg, Prešporok, Bratislava
1918	After World War I, following many centuries of Austro-Hungarian domination, Czechs and Slovaks were so thankful to American President Woodrow Wilson for supporting the establishment of their independent common state, Czechoslovakia, that they renamed Bratislava 'Wilsonovo Mesto' (Wilson City) but the new name didn't last for very long.
1919	Bratislava
2006	Young locals sometimes abbreviate the name to Blava

History

1809	Napoleonic troops besiege Bratislava
1811	A huge fire destroys Bratislava Castle
1818	The first steamboat on the Danube River
1840	Horse-drawn railway started running between Bratislava and Svätý Jur
1843	Ľudovít Štúr codifies Slovak literary language. Before, all literature was written in Czech
	King Ferdinand V signs the so-called Laws of March on abolition of serfdom in the Mirror Hall of the Primate's Palace
1848	Last session of the Hungarian Parliament in Bratislava
1848–49	Hungarian revolution against Habsburgs
1849	The Slovak National Council developed as the first representative Slovak political body in modern history. Its members spend 1849 co-operating with imperial Vienna to effect the separation of Slovakia from Hungary.
1861	The Martin Memorandum issued in Martin, central Slovakia, urging the establishment of a Slovak district and language within Greater Hungary
1863	Creation of Matica Slovenská (Little Mother of the Slovaks), a cultural and educational foundation
1867	Formation of Dual Monarchy (Austro-Hungarian). Slovaks subject to ruthless Magyarisation (Magyarosítás).

Contexts

1886	The present Slovak National Theatre built on the site of the Theatre of Estates
1891	Opening of the first bridge 'Old Bridge' over the Danube
1895	The first tram runs in Bratislava
1918	Bratislava becomes the administrative centre of Slovakia in the first Czechoslovak state, proclaimed a republic on 28 October 1918. Tomáš Masaryk becomes the first president, after the Pittsburgh Agreement in May 1918. **30 October** Martin Declaration. The Slovak National Council votes to federate with the Czechs (they hadn't been informed of events two days earlier in Prague!).
1919	**1 January** Occupation of the town by Czechoslovak legions and its annex to the Czechoslovak Republic. The city's name is changed from Pressburg (German) and Pozsony (Hungarian) to Bratislava.
1938	**November** Czech President Edvard Beneš lets the Germans take Czech lands; Slovaks declare desire for autonomy
1939	**14 March** Slovakia forced to declare itself a separate state, the day before Hitler makes Bohemia and Moravia a 'German protectorate'
1941	Jozef Tiso forms quasi-Nazi government, bans all opposition parties and deports 73,000 Jews to Nazi extermination camps
1944	Slovak National Uprising (SNP – Slovenské Narodné Povstanie) quashed by German army

History

1945	Collapse of Slovak State
	4 April Czechoslovakia 'liberated' by Red Army
1946	Foundation of Greater Bratislava by annexing the villages of Devín, Dúbravka, Lamač, Petržalka, Prievoz, Rača and Vajnory
1948	**February** The second Czechoslovak state was to be federal, but following communist takeover, administration is centralised in Prague
1968	**5 January** Alexander Dubček replaces Novotny as Party boss (Prague Spring, granting Czechs and Slovaks equal rights)
	21 August Russian tanks roll into Prague, Bratislava and other towns, and quash everything except the declaration on paper of separate but federated Czech and Slovak states. However, the power remains in Prague.
1969	**30 October** Agreement on the Czechoslovak Federation signed at Bratislava Castle. Bratislava gains official status as the capital of Slovakia.
1971	Bratislava grows as villages of Čunovo, Devínska Nová Ves, Jarovce, Podunajské Biskupice, Rusovce, Vrakuňa and Záhorská Bystrica are annexed
1989	**27 November** General strike of citizens of the town, supporting the movements Public against Violence and Civic Forum as well as student movements, later known as the Velvet Revolution

Contexts

1993	**1 January** Velvet Divorce, foundation of the Republic of Slovakia
2004	**3 March** Slovakia finally joins NATO along with Slovenia, Bulgaria and Romania
	1 May Slovakia joins EU along with nine other new member states, mostly from central Europe
2008–09	Slovakia plans to adopt the euro

POLITICS

In May 1997, a referendum was held on **NATO** membership and also the method of choosing the president. Voting papers were tampered with and Mečiar's boorish replies to reporters resulted in Slovakia being removed from the first group of east European countries lining up to join the **EU** or **NATO**.

Many Slovaks blamed the Mečiar government for not doing more to join the EU, by far Slovakia's largest trading partner after the Czech Republic. Slovaks were less upset by the rebuff from NATO; only 46% had voted to join the organisation in the 1997 referendum. Immediately following the EU announcement, President Kováč called for Mečiar's resignation and demanded early elections. Mečiar however managed to hang on until the elections in September 1998.

At the 1998 elections, Mečiar's HZDS won the largest percentage of the vote but were unable to form a government and so lost out to the right-wing coalition of **SDKU** (Slovak Democratic and Christian Union), led by Prime Minister **Mikuláš Dzurinda**.

On 16 October 2002 the SDKU coalition won a second term in office, when **President Rudolf Schuster** appointed a new Slovak government headed by Prime Minister Mikulaš Dzurinda. The coalition comprises three centre-right parties in addition to the SDKU: the SMK (party of the Hungarian Coalition), the KDH (Christian Democratic Movement) and the liberal party ANO (New Citizens' Alliance). The SDKU has six members in the government, the SMK has four and the KDH and ANO both have three.

The three right-wing parties are neither nationalist nor populist (unlike Mečiar) but instead remain a faithful friend of the West, and follow the part-liberal, part-conservative economic policy worked out by **Ivan Miklós** and his team at the Finance Ministry in Bratislava. The opposition is made up of the HZDS, SMER (Direction) and the KSS (Communist Party of Slovakia). Other political parties include the Free Forum, the HZD (Movement for Democracy), the HZDS-LS (Mečiar's branching-off Movement for a Democratic Slovakia–People's Party), the LU (People's Union) and the SNS (Slovak National Party).

On 15 June 2004, **Ivan Gasparovič** replaced Schuster as President of the Republic of Slovakia. This produced some nervous reactions, as while Rudolf Schuster was a former communist official 15 years ago, Ivan Gasparovič was the right-hand man of Vladimir Mečiar until just a few years ago.

The president of the republic is elected directly by the citizens and remains in office for five years. The 150 members of the Slovak parliament and the government are elected for a four-year term. The next elections are expected in September 2006.

Dzurinda's sensible, West-looking government put the country back on track with the rest of Europe and the country was let back into the exclusive **EU/NATO wannabes club**. On 3 March 2004, Slovakia joined **NATO** along with Slovenia, Bulgaria and Romania, and on I May 2004, Slovakia joined the European Union along with nine other states in the largest expansion in EU history.

New friends, old enemies

Mečiar's brutish populist stance had not helped relations with the neighbours. A law passed in 1995 recognised Slovak as the only official language, meaning that officially the large Hungarian minority could not use their mother tongue in public places. A separate law was passed in 1995 to protect the Slovak Republic, and allowed for the arrest of anyone criticising the government.

On the other side of the fence, the 1998–2002 right-wing Fidesz-led government in Hungary did little to endear themselves to the Slovaks, especially with the Status Law, promoted by Hungarian Prime Minister Viktor Orbán, which promised dual nationality and extra benefits for all Hungarians living beyond Hungary's borders. In a 2004 referendum, Hungarians voted against offering dual citizenship to ethnic Hungarians outside Hungary. The constant bickering has only abated since both countries joined the EU and both have more sober, forward-looking governments.

The Slovaks and Czechs continue to argue over the repercussions following the Velvet Divorce, in which Slovakia feels it came off worse. Slovaks always felt like the

Politics

neglected little sister in the federal Czechoslovakia, but now they are overtaking the Czech Republic in economic reforms and progress.

ECONOMY
The Tatra Tiger

In recent years, Slovakia's booming economy has become the envy of the region. Dubbed the 'Tatra Tiger' after the mountains in the north and spiritual symbol of the country, Slovakia's economy was a slow starter after the Velvet Divorce from the Czech Republic (1 January 1993) but has now taken off.

Slovakia mastered much of the difficult transition from a centrally planned economy to a modern market economy and came out smelling of roses. The Dzurinda government, spearheaded by Finance Minister Ivan Miklós made excellent progress during 2001–04 in macroeconomic stabilisation and structural reform. Major privatisations are nearly complete, the banking sector is almost entirely in foreign hands, and the government has helped facilitate a foreign investment boom with business-friendly policies, such as the labour market liberalisation.

However, the most attractive measure was on 1 January 2004, when the government replaced the income, corporate and sales taxes with a 19% flat tax rate, dramatically changing the economic landscape of the entire region and luring many international companies away from neighbouring countries. Slovakia now has one of the best investment environments in Europe. Taking into account the total tax burden, Slovakia has the lowest taxes of all of the EU and OECD countries.

The labour force is highly educated with 93% of Slovaks enjoying secondary or higher education and wages are still relatively low. The infrastructure is good, with both transport and communication easy as Slovakia is at the geographical heart of the new Europe. The Slovak workforce is 38.4% industry (processing, mining), 6.3% agriculture, with the remaining 55.3% working in the service industry.

Despite the general slowdown throughout Europe, Slovakia's economic growth exceeded expectations in 2001–04. Unemployment remains at an unacceptable 16% but the figure is decreasing, while the GDP (25.44 billion euros) is on the up, and inflation is a steady 3.3%. According to the World Bank, Slovakia had the fastest transforming business environment in the world in 2004, and already comparisons are being drawn between the Tatra Tiger and Ireland's Celtic Tiger economic transformation in the 1990s.

Foreign investment was expected to total about 2.2 billion euros in 2005, twice the amount attracted in the previous year. The government's reform of the labour code makes Slovakia attractive for foreign companies by creating a more flexible working environment than in western Europe. Hiring and firing is easier and companies can demand longer working hours.

In recent years, multi-nationals such as IBM, Johnson Controls, Fujitsu, Samsung, Coca-Cola, Whirlpool, Henkel, Siemens, Heineken and South Africa Breweries have launched operations in Slovakia; however, the biggest investments have been in car plants. A huge car manufacturing plant for Peugeot-Citroen has sprung up in less than a year, just 50km from Bratislava. Volkswagen is already present, but soon it will

Economy

be joined by Kia Motors, Ford Motors and Hyundai and in less than two years, Slovakia is expected to produce more cars per head than any other country in the world.

The only part of Slovakia not benefiting from this boom is the far east of the country which still suffers from poor infrastructure and unemployment reaching 20%. It takes more than five hours to get to the isolated east by bus, whereas Vienna is less than an hour by car and Budapest just under two hours. Slovakia hopes to use EU funds to develop the far east regions. The service industry needs to be overhauled and the country's natural treasures will be improved to develop tourism.

EU membership

Slovakia joined the EU on 1 May 2004 along with nine other mostly central European countries.

Countries like Slovakia, Poland, Hungary and the Czech Republic are at present less wealthy than most other EU countries, but they are catching up fast. Slovakia's GDP per inhabitant was 45% of the EU average in 2001, but the percentage was double that of the previous year, demonstrating the thriving nature of the Slovak economy. Slovakia, along with the other new EU members, contributes just 4% towards the EU's economy. Experts predict that this will grow as more investors start looking eastwards.

The information society in Slovakia is also catching up. Figures for 2001 show ownership of 15 PCs per 100 people in Slovakia, whereas the EU average was 31 per 100 people. As for cell phones, in 2001, 54% of Slovaks owned a mobile phone, although that figure has grown at a spectacular rate since then. In May 2003, a Eurobarometer survey asked a representative survey of people in the EU candidate countries whether EU membership was a good or bad thing; 59% of Slovaks said it was good, while 5% were negative about the EU. This result was one of the more positive in the survey.

The real change will come when Slovakia joins the euro mechanism and prices alter radically. Slovakia hopes to join the European monetary system in 2006–07 and introduce the euro in 2008–09.

PEOPLE

Slovaks embody the stereotype of Slavic hospitality, tempered by a generous portion of dour realism. However, they are neither grumpy like their Hungarian neighbours nor uptight like the Austrians over the river. Slovaks welcome visitors with open arms, and usually an open bottle. Then there's the legendary razor-cheekboned beauty of Slovak females, deriving from a fascinatingly exotic gene pool. Many top models are from Slovakia.

The difference in atmosphere between Bratislava and Vienna or Budapest is marked. It may be because Bratislava is smaller and more manageable but the people are more relaxed and have more time to sit and enjoy a coffee, beer or glass of Slovak wine at one of the hundreds of terrace cafés in the Mediterranean-style capital. However, it's not all rosé in Europe's newest capital.

Slovaks have massive chips on their shoulders about the Czechs, and with reason. Only recently has the dynamic Slovak economy allowed them to hold their heads high in the region after years of being treated like a problematic little sister. It still rankles that most people think the greatest stars of Czechoslovak ice hockey, football and Olympic teams of the past were Czech, as many were Slovak.

Bratislava locals are a brainy lot. Imagine living in a town where often old Pressburg families have three first languages, and not the easy ones either; Slovak, Hungarian and German are widely spoken. Situated strategically at the meeting point of three countries, three cultures and three languages, Bratislava can take the best of everything and has developed a cosmopolitan outlook, adapting well to its new EU member status.

There is quite a lot of jealousy from other parts of the country that Bratislava gets the best of everything. Bratislava is closer to Vienna than to many other Slovak cities, in terms of both geography and attitude. Towns in the far east feel neglected and there is a problem of demographics as almost all students leave to study in Bratislava then decide to stay there, causing a brain drain in towns further east and a desperate housing shortage in the capital.

Around 600,000 ethnic Hungarians live in Slovakia, mostly in the south and east of the country. The Slovak Constitution of 1992 guarantees the rights of minorities and most Hungarian children receive education in their mother tongue. Politically, Slovakia and Hungary are always arguing; in private Slovaks and Hungarians get along fine. However in 1996, the Mečiar government did not help relations by making Slovak the only official language, revenge perhaps for ruthless Magyarisation in the past.

The Roma are the second largest minority group and it is estimated that as many as half a million live mostly in the neglected eastern regions with no amenities, high unemployment and almost no schooling. Under communism, everybody had to have a job, but now potential employers can openly display their prejudices and reject Roma workers. Roma children are tested in Slovak instead of their own language then dumped in 'special schools'. On the Roma side, integration into Slovak society is also difficult because of the complicated caste system and community ties.

In World War II, 80,000 Slovak Roma escaped extermination because the Germans only occupied Slovakia after the Slovak National Uprising (SNP) in 1942. The communists provided homes and jobs for the Roma, but in the process destroyed their nomadic lifestyle.

The Ruthene minority live in the Slovakian far east, on the border with Ukraine. They have a distinct yet dying culture as many young people leave to find work elsewhere.

The **ethnic make up** of Slovakia is 85.8% Slovak, 9.7% Hungarian, 1.7% Roma (although the Roma community is continually under-reported, and estimated at more than 500,000), 0.8% Czech, 0.4% Ruthene, 0.2% Ukrainian, 0.1% German, 0.1% Polish (1.2% other).

People

CULTURAL ETIQUETTE
Get up, stand up

On trams, trolleybuses and buses, it is expected that young people and men will stand up and give their seat to an elderly traveller or pregnant woman. If they don't notice, it will be pointed out by all those in surrounding seats and severe chastisement will follow.

Czecho-Slovenia

Be sensitive to the fact that Slovakia has always played second fiddle to the Czech Republic (never even getting its own guidebook until Bradt) and remember the difference between Slovakia and Slovenia. Nationals of both countries are equally irritated by the Western media's (CNN, BBC, *USA Today*) and President G W Bush's apparent inability to tell these two very different countries apart.

Formalities

Office workers and civil servants can be very formal when addressing colleagues. Older-generation workers insist on using 'Pani' (Mrs) or 'Pan' (Mr) plus the surname even if they've known the person for years, and the colleague is younger (but more important).

'Slečna' (Miss) is also used. The polite 'Vy' (thou) is also used instead of the familiar 'ty' (you). Foreigners attempting to speak Slovak should use the formal version to be safe, until told otherwise.

Oxygen phobia

Don't open a window on the tram, even in the height of summer; fresh air is dangerous in draught form. Also, if you have a small child, make sure you take a hat and scarf to Bratislava for them, even in midsummer, or you risk incurring the wrath of Slovak grannies berating you for endangering your tiny tot's health.

Greetings

It is customary to say hello and goodbye when entering/leaving a shop, lift, office or quiet café. To enter without a word is considered ill-mannered. There are many ways of saying hello and goodbye in Bratislava. *Dobrý deň* is used with elderly neighbours, business associates, waiters and shop assistants.

Ruky bozkávam (I kiss your hands) is a very formal greeting which melts grannies' hearts.

Dovidenia is the polite goodbye, though the more final *zbohom* (adieu) can be used.

Dopočutia (until I hear you next) is used to say goodbye on the phone.

Ahoj and *čau* are the most common informal greetings. These words serve as both hello and goodbye. *Ahoj* (me hearties) sounds like it came from sailors.

Servus comes from the Latin 'I serve' and is also popular in Hungary.

Home visits

If lucky enough to be invited to a Slovak home, take a gift. Alcohol always goes down well – a bottle of excellent local white wine, Slivovica (plum brandy) or the gin-like

Cultural etiquette

Borovička. Chocolates and flowers are welcome with the hostess, but don't take dried flowers or even-numbered bunches as these have a morbid significance. You will probably be expected to remove your shoes at the door and don grandpa's old slippers.

GIVING SOMETHING BACK
Local charities

Bratislava Groove at **UFO Watch Taste Groove** Nový most; ✆ 02 6252 0300; e info@u-f-o.sk; www.u-f-o.sk. A campaign run by the brand new restaurant/nightclub to help abandoned children growing up in orphanages. The cover charge for Groove (the party every Saturday night) is 150Sk, 30Sk of which goes to the orphanages in a non-profit project. Supporters receive and wear a three-coloured wristband.

Food not Bombs Charity (Jedlo namiesto zbraní) Local contacts in Bratislava: Mlynské Nivy 41; ✆/f 02 5542 2176; e mail@jedlo.sk; www.jedlo.sk

International Women's Club (IWC) of Bratislava meets in room 171; Hotel Danube; Rybné námestie 1; charity co-ordinator Karen Ochotnicka; e charity@iwc.sk; www.iwc.sk

Nota Bene OZ Proti prude, Karpatská 10; ✆/f 02 5262 5962; e protiprudu@notabene.sk; www.nota-bene.sk. A *Big Issue*-style magazine for the homeless to sell. *Nota Bene* is a member of INSP, the International Network of Street Papers, a global association of over 45 street papers in 27 countries around the world. Launched in 1994 by *The Big Issue*, INSP now has a combined monthly sales figure of over 2 million. *Nota Bene* in Bratislava is supported by local celebrities and actors.

Red Cross (Slovenský Cervený Kríž) Grösslingova 24; ℡ 02 5292 5305; f 02 5292 3279; www.redcross.sk

Sloboda Zvierat (Freedom for Animals) Mlynské Nivy 37; ℡ 02 5442 4033; www.slobodazvierat.sk (also PO Box 35, 814 99 Bratislava). Founded on 10 August 1992, it provides two shelters for the many stray dogs and cats. They also campaign against the long-distance transportation across Europe of live animals, against cruel farming methods, bears kept in captivity and animal experimentation. Shelters are at Polianky 8, open daily 10.00–18.00, ℡ 02 16187 (or m 0903 727 015) and at Rožňavská cesta, open daily 14.00–18.00.

Unicef also operates in Bratislava; Grösslingová 6, PO Box 52, Bratislava 810 00; ℡ 02 5296 5082, 5296 1930; f 02 5296 5084; e natcom@unicef.sk; www.unicef.sk; bank a/c No: 4 000 915 305/3100

Usmev ako dar (Smile as a gift) Ševčenkova 21; ℡ 02 6381 5209; www.usmev.sk; bank a/c No: 4040 029 105 / 3100. Organisation for orphans to 'let every child have a family'. There is a strange law in Slovakia that doesn't allow a child to be adopted if the real parent visits the children's home at least once a month, preventing many adoptions. Usmev ako dar is the oldest and the biggest voluntary organisation for the support of abandoned children in Slovakia. Manager: Bruno Biscontini.

BUSINESS

Bratislava's excellent strategic location at the meeting point of Slovakia, Austria and Hungary makes it a popular destination for business travellers and international business conferences. The city is served by two airports, Bratislava and Vienna, giving more possibilities for flights. Bratislava is also accessible by motorway or even by boat or hydrofoil along the Danube.

Bratislava bulges with three- and four-star hotels, specialised 'business hotels' with superb facilities, such as WiFi (Wireless Fidelity) in every room and state-of-the-art technical equipment.

Business etiquette is similar to that of western Europe, the only difference being the central European mania for handing out business cards like confetti at a wedding. The language of business is English, although most Slovaks are equally at home in German; some older people speak Russian although they may not be too happy about speaking it. Slovaks can also get by on a passive level in most of the other Slavic tongues and many people speak Hungarian as well. Slovaks and Czechs can easily understand each other and the linguistic differences to a foreign ear are minimal. Don't feel intimidated linguistically by their superior powers; Slovak businesspeople are charming and relaxed and will happily adapt to your needs.

To maintain effective business relations, you should have regular face-to-face meetings, and remember to dress conservatively for official meetings; use surnames and formalities such as Mr and Mrs until invited to use first names. Don't even think of arranging a business meeting during the holiday months of July and August and also be aware that most companies shut down between 24 December and 2 January.

The usual business hours are 09.00–17.00, although don't expect to find any government workers still in their offices after 15.00 on a Friday afternoon. Banks operate 08.00–17.00, Monday–Thursday and 08.00–15.00 on Friday. Shops usually open 08.00–18.00 and close at midday on Saturday, but some malls are open all weekend.

Useful contacts

American Chamber of Commerce (CEO Jake Sleger) Rybné námestie 1; ☏ 02 5464 0534; e office@amcham.sk; www.amcham.sk

British Chamber of Commerce (CEO Lívia Eperjesiová) Sedlárska 5; ☏ 02 5292 0371; e director@britcham.sk; www.britcham.sk

Slovak–Australian Chamber of Commerce (CEO Daniel Andráško) Jégeho 8; ☏ 02 5564 2853; www.sachamber.sk

Slovak–Austrian Chamber of Commerce Kutlíková 17, PO Box 228; ☏ 02 6353 6787; e sohk@sohk.sk; www.sohk.sk

Slovak Chamber of Commerce and Industry Gorkého 9; ☏ 02 5443 3291; e sopkurad@sopk.sk; www.sopk.sk

Ministry of the Economy www.economy.gov.sk

Ministry of Finance www.finance.gov.sk

Slovak Government www.vlada.gov.sk/english/

Bratislava Stock Exchange www.bsse.sk

Incheba (www.incheba.sk) is the huge exhibition and convention site just over the river in Petržalka.

Business

The internet version of **The Book of Lists** (*www.greenpages.sk*) produced by the *Slovak Spectator* has numerous business contacts: accountants, banks, couriers, embassies, consulates, language schools, security firms, shipping, law firms, real estate, health care; you name it, they've listed it. *The Book of Lists 2005* is the sixth edition and costs 149Sk or US$15 abroad.

RELIGION

Some 69% of Slovaks say they are Roman Catholic, although in practice they are not as fervent as their northern neighbours, the Poles, and are rather more enthusiastic than the Magyars to the south. Young Slovaks are also more devout than the Czechs. The Roman Catholic Church is the largest in Slovakia followed by the Evangelical Church of the Augsburg Confession and the Greek-Catholic Church. The first Christian church in Slovakia was founded in AD833 in the city of Nitra.

Orthodox and Greek-Catholic believers are found in the north and east of the country, where the Orthodox icons resemble those of Russia. The beautiful wooden churches of Ruthenia in eastern Slovakia hold Greek-Catholic/Orthodox treasures.

The late Pope John Paul II visited Bratislava in 1990, 1995 and 2002, and the city is one of the few in the world which His

Holiness visited three times. His last visit to Bratislava in 2002 drew vast crowds to Sad Janka Kráľa (park) on the southern side of the Danube.

The new fifth bridge in Bratislava has just been constructed, with the working title of Košická Bridge, but the local daily paper, *Pravda*, ran a poll for the public's choice of name and Pope John Paul II Bridge was the overwhelming winner. The City Council then conducted a new poll asking voters not to choose a person because they couldn't agree. The winning name was the Apollo Bridge, after a nearby refinery.

Until World War II, the Jews played a significant role in Bratislava's multi-national, multi-cultural population. According to the Jewish Museum, there is evidence Jewish merchants operated in the Roman province of Kvadia, now Slovakia. After the anti-Jewish riots in western Europe in the 11th century, many Jews found refuge in Bratislava and during the Middle Ages the Jewish community had established itself, with certain privileges and rights. In 1750, some 15,000 Jews lived in Bratislava, in a ghetto between the town walls and Castle Hill. Židovska ulica (Jewish Street) still recalls part of this district. Bratislava was a centre of Jewish Orthodox education, led by rabbi Mose Schreiber (Chatam Sofer, whose mausoleum can be visited, see page 209) and a yeshiva founded in 1806 was the only university in the city.

When Slovakia allied itself to Hitler's Germany, around 74,000 Slovak Jews were deported, the survivors emigrated and today only 2,000 remain in the entire country, 800 in Bratislava. At one time there were 29 synagogues in Bratislava. The main synagogue and much of the Jewish district was demolished to make way for the construction of the Nový Most (New Bridge) and Staromestská main road that slices between the Old Town and the castle. Today, one synagogue can be found on Heydukova ulica and there is a large cemetery to the west of town.

Like most post-communist countries in the region, Slovakia has its fair share of 'new' religions, moving into the supposed spiritual vacuum: Jehovah's Witnesses, Mormons, Baha'is, Hare Krishnas and Scientologists are all active in Bratislava.

CULTURE

Much as it pains them to admit it, Slovak history and culture, including literature, are bound up inextricably with that of Hungary.

From the 10th century until 1918, the country was Upper Country (Felvidék in Hungarian) and during the Middle Ages Czech was used alongside Hungarian, German and Latin. Surviving texts from the region, the earliest known being the 11th-century *Legends of Saints Svorak and Benedict*, are all in Latin. The earliest specimens of Czech vernacular are 15th-century town documents and devotional texts, such as the Špis Prayers from 1480. Magyar culture blossomed during the enlightened rule of Hungarian King Mátyás Corvinus, who founded the Academia Istropolitana in 1465.

There was much traditional folksong and balladry in the 17th and 18th centuries. A popular tale told of a real-life Robin Hood figure, Juraj Jánošík (1688–1713), who led a group of bandits in northern Slovakia and was executed in Liptovský Mikuláš main square. In 1787, Catholic priest and linguist Anton Bernolák published his *Grammatica Slavica* and in 1790 he created a massive six-volume dictionary of Slovak–Czech–Latin–German–Hungarian, published in 1827 after his death. In 1792 Bernolák helped found the Slovak Learned Society and stirred a national cultural awakening in the country. The first writer to use Bernolák's Slovak was Juraj Fándly, although more successful was another Catholic priest Ján Hollý (1785–1849) who translated Virgil's *Aeneid* and wrote on emotive Slovak–Slav themes such as the *Svatopluk* (1833) about the Moravian prince. Hollý is considered the founding father of Slovak poetry and there's a statue of him seated in a courtyard just behind St Martin's Cathedral.

In 1843, Ludovit Štúr codified the Slovak literary language. He started a Slovak-language daily paper in 1845 and in literature stressed the importance of local and original writers. Three poets, Janko Kráľ, Ján Botto and Andrej Sládkovič personified the folk romanticism of the Štúr generation. Kráľ was a strange, solitary figure who battled against the Hungarians. Sládkovič is best known for the long poem *Marína* inspired by an unhappy love affair.

To learn more about life in the Slovak countryside, we can also turn to the eccentric Hungarian author Kálmán Mikszáth (1847–1910) who described life in Felvidék with a gentle ironic humour. His novel *The Siege of Beszterce* ('Beszterce ostroma' in Hungarian) appears surprisingly contemporary in theme.

Oppressed by the Hungarian language, Slovak writers found more success in poetry. The lawyer Pavol Országh Hviezdoslav (1849–1921) was the most creative of

Culture

the period. His acclaimed long narrative poem *Hájnikova žena* (The Gamekeeper's Wife) celebrates the freedom of the countryside opposed to the moral corruption of some of the aristocracy. In the years preceding World War I, a group known as the 'Slovak Literary Moderna' appeared with Ivan Krasko at the forefront, describing atmospheric, melancholic moods. After World War II, Stalinism restricted creativity with its emphasis on dreary Socialist Realism. Ladislav Mňačko became the leading Slovak literary dissident describing the life of a corrupt communist politician in *Ako chutí moc* (The Taste of Power) in 1967. Klára Jarunková, born 1922, is one of the few female writers to be translated from Slovak. Her teenage novels have a psychological sensitivity and fresh charm. A book to look out for is by Martin Šimečka, the son of a well-known Bratislava-based Czech dissident writer Milan Šimečka. His autobiographical novel *Džin* was translated as *Year of the Frog*.

As for music, Bratislava was visited by many of the greats: Mozart, Haydn, Barťok, Liszt and Beethoven, many of whom studied within the Old Town walls and gave concerts. Home-grown music star Johann Nepomuk Hummel (1778–1837) was a disciple of Mozart and Haydn and a friend to Beethoven and Paganini. The piano virtuoso, composer and world-famous music teacher created music in many styles and the house where he was born can be visited (at Klobúčnicka 2). In the 18th century, Slovaks wanted to redefine their folk-music heritage and composers used folk motifs in classical compositions. Mikuláš Schneider-Trnavský and Ján Levoslav Bela were the most well known. Communism stifled modern music in the second half of the 20th century, although there was a significant jazz movement, led in the

1960s by bands such as Combo 4, the Bratislava Jazz Quartet, the Medik Quintet and Traditional Club Bratislava. Jazz clubs are popular in Bratislava today and there are many places to hear live music. Rock and pop artists are popular with singers such as Paľo Habera and his former band, Team. Reggae (*www.reggae.sk*) is also thriving in the Slovak capital alongside ambient music, death metal and the inevitable techno. The most popular programme on Slovak television recently was *Superstar*, a singing talent contest along the lines of *Pop Idol*.

Perhaps because of the diversity of influences on the land – Celtic, Roman, Hungarian, Slavic German and others – Slovakia has a remarkably varied folk-song and dance heritage. The *fujara* is an instrument unique to Slovakia that looks like a didgeridoo but is played like a flute. The folk revivalist Tibor Koblíček uses many folk styles on his album *My Dear Pipes*, using the mournful drone of the *fujara*, the hurdy gurdy and other traditional instruments.

For visual arts, a trip to the Slovak National Gallery reveals the wealth of early religious painting from the region. Pavol of Levoča was the most outstanding Gothic sculptor. Baroque art by painters such as Ján Kracker and Jakub Bogdan is found in churches across the country. The 19th-century Slovak National Revival threw up a crop of Slovak painters. The solitary, strange Hungarian painter Ladislav Medňanský was born in Beckov in what is now Slovakia in 1850. He depicted the vivid Slovak landscapes and lives of tramps and poor people with great power. Many of his powerful paintings can be seen at the Slovak National Gallery. Under communism, statues were chunky Soviet constructivist. Július Bártfay created numerous World War II monuments, including the Slavín Monument. Nowadays, Bratislava is bulging with private galleries, many of which have artwork for sale. Check out the list on page 214 (*Museums and sightseeing* section) for places to spot a new Slovak master, or mistress.

NATIONAL HOLIDAYS AND FEAST DAYS

Businesses and shops close for national holidays.

Festivals and events

Bratislava celebrates a range of events throughout the year. Tickets and more information are available from the BKIS office at Klobučnícka 2; www.bkis.sk. The City Hall website www.bratislava.sk also has details of events. Where a specific festival anniversary is quoted, this refers to that due in 2006.

ITF Slovakia Tour (26–29 Jan) The 12th International Travel Fair. Held annually at Incheba, Bratislava's huge exhibition and convention site. See www.incheba.sk.

City Ball (Feb each year) Out come the glad rags as Bratislava's high society puts on its finery and trips the light fantastic at the Reduta. See www.reduta.sk for more details. Carnivals also occur in February.

Mozart Week (around 15–23 Feb) The ninth year of the International Festival of music by Mozart and his contemporaries with accompanying events at the Slovak Philharmonic, organised by the Austrian Centre of Culture. See www.filharm.sk.

Passion Plays (around end of Mar) Passion plays take place in St Martin's Cathedral and on the Main Square (Hlavné námestie).

National Running Race Devín–Bratislava (around 10 Apr) For the last 56 years, the Bratislava people have been celebrating the arrival of spring with a national race from Devín to Bratislava, a distance of 12.33km. This is the oldest still-running race in the country. In 2000, the International Olympic Committee included this race on its list of the most significant running events in Europe. En route, you might spot keen runner Mikuláš Dzurinda who has completed more than 20 marathons in the last 12 years. He is the first serving prime minister to compete in the London marathon.

The 16th Annual Wine Exhibition (around 10–11 Apr) The winegrowers' club of Svätý Jur, near Bratislava, presents its annual show. Call for more details, ↘ 02 4497 1427.

Wine Fair (around 16–17 Apr) The 11th international competition, exhibition and enthusiastic tasting of wines at the Culture House of Pezinok, near Bratislava. For more information see the town's own website www.pezinok.sk.

Bratislava for Everybody (22–23 Apr) At this time of year, the Bratislava local government arranges a series of open days, so everyone can check up on the work, activities and services of the town and its organisations. The date is historical as the mayor of Bratislava was traditionally elected on 24 April, based on a charter by Kind

András III who granted Bratislava many municipal privileges. During the weekend nearest that date, most city services such as museums and galleries are open and there is no admission charge.

Flóra Bratislava (26 Apr–1 May) The 27th international fair of flowers and garden technology at the fair complex of Incheba on the right-hand embankment of the Danube River. For more than a quarter of a century, Bratislava has been filled with the heady aroma of fresh flowers at the end of April.

The Turza Craftsmen Fair at Červený Kameň (around 1 May) The sixth annual meeting of craftsmen. The market makes a fitting end to the event. Also there is a presentation of national costumes and customs. See www.snm.sk/ck.

Days of Europe Bratislava (around 1–9 May) An international festival of music, film, dance, fine art and fun. Contact the Culture House (Dom kultúry); ☏ 09 383 6764.

Cycling Tour of Friendship (around 21 May) You'll need a passport for this cycling event. Cyclists from the region set off on a 90km bike ride through Austria, Hungary and back to Bratislava.

Challenge Day (around 26 May) The 13th year of an international competition involving all kinds of sports and activities.

St Urban's Day in Pezinok (around 27 May) A celebration of the patron saint of wine-growing. A wine-lovers' meeting with music, and homage to the statues of St Urban. See www.museumpezinok.sk.

Children's Day at Červený Kameň (around 30 May) A fun day out for all the family at the imposing castle near Bratislava. See www.snm.sk/ck for details.

Children's Day (around 1 Jun) On this day, Bratislava belongs to children. A range of entertainment for children on stages throughout the Old Town with performances, theatre, concerts and sports events.

Beer Festival-Junifest (2–11 Jun) Beer will flow freely for ten days at the Incheba exhibition and congress centre. The pivný festival is the biggest beer festival in Slovakia. See www.incheba.sk.

International Festival of Water Sprites (around 4 Jun) A collection of attractions celebrating water, culminating in a procession and declaration of the best water sprite, apprentice, journeyman, master and family, filling up the city centre with watery delights. Water sprites wearing masks will gambol about the town.

The Opening of the Season of the Malokarpatská Wine Route (around 11 Jun) The wine season on the Small Carpathian Wine Route gets off to a flying start with this festival at Svätý Jur, near Bratislava.

Cultural Summer 2006 (around 17 Jun–1 Aug) A feast of music, dance, singing, crafts, amusements and gastronomic delights in Bratislava. The 31st annual international summer festival of art and culture takes place throughout the city. Classical music concerts, fanfare concerts, chansons, the Guitar Festival, the Organ

Music Days and the Festival of Children's Folk Ensembles are all part of this huge festival of culture. There are performances and happenings in all the squares, and sculptures are exhibited in the gardens and courtyards of the city. Another event is entitled Bratislava Ghosts and Monsters and there is also a Fiesta Latina which blends in well with the Mediterranean ambience in the Old Town.

Castle Festivities of Bratislava (around 18 Jun–3 Sep) An international festival of arts and culture. For 13 weekends, the main courtyard of the castle is the scene of a series of concerts, classical and contemporary music. There are also Organ Music Days, a summer Shakespeare theatre and many other performances.

Festival of Historic Fencing (around 12–13 Jul) A historic show with an accompanying cultural programme at Červený Kameň. See www.snm.sk/ck.

Knightly Games at Červený Kameň Castle (around 21–22 Aug) A presentation of the art of knights, accompanied by more cultural programmes. See www.snm.sk/ck.

The Červený Kameň Ramble (around end of Aug) A social event and walk taking place around the huge castle. See www.snm.sk/ck.

Days of Masters of Úľuv (around 2–3 Sep) Úľuv is an organisation which specialises in folk art production, traditional crafts and specialist collaborations. It has its own network of retail shops with a good selection of embroidered items, colourful folk costumes, woollen fabrics, glass painting, Easter eggs and wooden crafts. A market and fair will showcase the items in front of the Primate's Palace in Bratislava.

Coronation Festivities (around 3 Sep) Bratislava is once again the town of coronations. Actors in period costumes will take the solemn vows, make a regal procession through the Old Town, and celebrations end with the dubbing of knights and much merrymaking.

Vintage Festival in Rača (around 10–12 Sep) A celebration of wine with a show of grape processing, pressing and tasting. Rača is on the outskirts of Bratislava at the start of the Small Carpathian Wine Route. The Rača Winemakers' Society has more details; ☎ 0905 468 943 (cell phone).

Small Carpathian Vintage Festival at Pezinok (around 24–26 Sep) The event celebrates wine and winemaking. Check out www.pezinok.sk.

Music Festival of Bratislava/Bratislavské Hudobné Slávnosti (around 23 Sep–7 Oct) The most prestigious festival of classical music in Slovakia, now running for more than 40 years. Look at the Bratislava City Hall website at www.bratislava.sk for details of the 42nd year. An integral part of the festival is the international tribune of young concert masters.

Biennial of Illustrations Bratislava (all Oct, every even year) The International competition is an exhibition of illustrations of books for children and young people.

ART exhibition (around 18–22 Oct) The sixth international art exhibition at Incheba. See www.incheba.sk.

Bratislava Jazz Days (around 21–23 Oct) The international jazz festival is one of the most popular events of its kind in central Europe. It takes place at the PKO cultural centre on the banks of the Danube. See www.bjd.sk.

Photography Month (Nov) An annual celebration of photography at venues all over Bratislava.

Christmas Market (around 25 Nov–23 Dec) One of the most popular events in Bratislava. The Christmas Market fills the Main Square with stalls offering traditional arts and crafts. Visitors can keep up their strengths with a range of food and drink on offer, from bread with lard and onion to potato pancakes with goose liver or sweet pancakes with poppy and walnuts or apple pie, all washed down with hot mulled wine, festive punch or a special hot and heady drink, *hriatô* (mead).

International Film Festival (around 2–10 Dec) The eighth film festival has a competition of first and second feature films, plus a selection of European films, independent cimema, premieres, profiles, free zones and a series of films showing outside the competition. For more details, look at www.iffbratislava.sk.

St Nicholas's Day and the Lighting of the Christmas Tree (6 Dec) An event to celebrate St Mikuláš with presents and lots of chocolate for the children.

Christmas in the Castle (Dec) Full-day programmes devoted to Christmas events for children. The website of the National Museum, www.snm-hm.sk, has more details.

New Year's Eve Party in the City (31 Dec) New Year's Eve in Bratislava has a unique atmosphere. Around 50,000 people gather in the tiny Old Town centre and are joined by several thousand tourists to enjoy live concerts, open-air discos and other cultural events. The climax is the midnight fireworks show over the Danube and the luminous animations on the river embankment.

National and public holidays
1 January	New Year's Day and Anniversary of the Establishment of the Slovak Republic in 1993
5 July	St Cyril and Methodius Day
29 August	Anniversary of the Slovak National Uprising
1 September	Slovak Republic Constitution Day
17 November	Day of Struggle against Totalitarianism/Fight for Democracy

Feast days
6 January	Epiphany, Three Magi, Orthodox Christmas
March/April	Good Friday
March/April	Easter Monday

1 May	Labour Day
8 May	Victory against Fascism Day – end of World War II
15 September	Holy Mary, Our Lady of Sorrows, Patron Saint of Slovakia
1 November	All Saints' Day
24 December	Christmas Eve
25 December	Christmas Day
26 December	St Stephen's Day

GEOGRAPHY

The Republic of Slovakia occupies a territory of 48,845km², is landlocked and surrounded by five countries: Austria, Czech Republic, Poland, Ukraine and Hungary. The border of 1,611.5km divides up thus: Austria 115.3km, Czech Republic 261.3km, Poland 508.2km, Ukraine 95.8km, Hungary 630.9km. Despite the distance from the sea, Slovakia has many lakes, streams and rivers and 45km² of its total territory is covered by water. Slovakia is situated at 16°50–22°34'E and 47°42–49°37'N. The mountain peak of Krahule (1,062m), near Banská Bystríca in central Slovakia is considered the geographical centre of Europe and more than 80% of the country sits at over 750m above sea level.

Bratislava is Slovakia's capital and is situated at the western tip of the country, in a highly strategic position on the mighty Danube River at the meeting point of three countries: Slovakia, Austria and Hungary. The state border with Austria is just over the Danube River from Bratislava, within walking distance of the town centre.

The state border with Hungary is just 16km away, just beyond Bratislava city limits. The Danube flows through Bratislava dividing the historic Old Town centre from the modern housing district of Petržalka.

The most important river is the Danube (Dunaj), the river route connecting Slovakia with the harbours of the Black Sea and, through the Rhine–Main–Danube waterway, with west European harbours. In the past, two significant trade arteries led through Slovakia: the Amber (Jantarova) and Czech routes, along which not only goods (gold, amber, fur) used to flow, but also information, which enabled mutual knowledge of, and understanding between, particular peoples and countries. Today, Slovakia is becoming an important junction of economic and commercial relations between eastern and western Europe.

CLIMATE

Slovakia's climate is temperate with warm, wet summers and cold, hard winters. Bratislava is located in a mild climatic zone of continental nature, characterised by wide differences between temperatures in summer and winter, as well as by four distinct seasons of the year. Average temperatures in Bratislava for winter are -1–4°C (30–40°F), spring and autumn 9–21°C (49–69°F), summer 24–26°C (75–79°F) although in recent years, spring and autumn have merged into the more dramatic seasons, and spring, usually a delightful season in the Old Town, has sadly almost disappeared. Snow cover on the mountains in the north is less than it has been in the past. The lowest annual temperature is in the mountains at Lomnicky Peak (-3.7°C). The warmest zone is the Podunajska Lowland (10.3°C).

For more information before you set off, ie: on whether to pack an extra jumper, look at www.meteo.sk.

NATURE

Bratislava is very green: a notice board by the castle lists many species of flora and fauna found in the city. Wildlife around the castle includes bats, butterflies, lizards, woodpeckers and red squirrels. There are also many varieties of wildflower and plant: Chinese wolfberry, houseleek, flowering onion, royal knight's spur, wild violets and Immortelle.

Bratislava has 809ha (2,020 acres) of parks and forests, 34 protected reservations. Most of this is formed by the Bratislavský lesov park (Bratislava Forest Park), to the north of the city. Despite centuries of deforestation and the effects of acid rain after burning brown coal, 40% of the country is still covered by forest, mainly beech and spruce. Arable land accounts for 30% of the country, while meadows and pastures cover 17%. Slovakia is less industrialised than the Czech Republic and its forests and rivers were less damaged by pollution.

The Gabčikovo-Nagymaros hydro-electric dam, situated 40km downstream from Bratislava, has been an environmental disaster on all sides. The idea was first mooted in 1977 by the communists of Czechoslovakia and Hungary and cynically supported by the Austrians, who also looked for cheap energy sources at another

Contexts

country's environmental expense. The Czechoslovak government was desperate to find another source of energy to replace the brown coal, whose pollution destroyed most of the country's forests. The Hungarian government pulled out in 1989 after protests by the green lobby, and called for an international inquiry into the environmental effects of the dam on the Danube. The Slovaks had already invested huge amounts of money and continued with a scaled-down version of the project, diverting part of the Danube in 1993. In 1997, the International Court at The Hague ruled in favour of Slovakia, but that Slovakia had acted illegally by diverting the river. The court ordered both sides to come up with a joint plan for the future of the project but the arguments wrangle on and the matter is no longer in the political limelight. Tragically, the environmental damage has already been done according to ecologists on both sides of the river. You can visit the site on a boat cruise or cycle along a new route from Bratislava.

Planning

BRATISLAVA – A PRACTICAL OVERVIEW

Central Bratislava is small, neat and compact and you will not find it easy to get lost. Having said that, the twisting, turning streets of the compact Old Town may get a bit confusing after sampling the excellent local brews!

Bratislava's Old Town and the castle are separated by the main road Staroméstská leading to the Nový most (New Bridge). To build this bridge and flyover section of the road in 1972, the Jewish synagogue and ghetto were demolished. The Danube runs along the side of the Old Town, flowing west to east as it passes through Bratislava.

The business area of Bratislava is situated to the east of the Old Town, as well as to the north, clustered around Námestie SNP although some banks and offices are found within the Old Town too.

The gruesome modern housing district of Petržalka spreads out in a vast concrete jungle on the southern side of the Danube, and the district is trapped in an enclave of Slovakia that lies between the Danube and the borders with Austria and Hungary.

Five bridges cross the Danube in Bratislava, the most recognisable being the Nový most (New Bridge) sometimes called SNP most. This bridge is also called the UFO Bridge by tourists because of the flying saucer space ship and UFO café that perches on top of the western column. The bridge's title of 'new bridge' will be usurped by a newer bridge when the Apollo Bridge opens as an elegant white arc across the river. You can still tread warily across the wooden slats of the Old (railway) Bridge linking the Old Town with Sad Janka Kráľa (park). Trams used to run across this bridge all the way to Vienna.

Bratislava's M R Štefánik Airport is located 9km northeast of the city and several top business hotels are found en route. Many people find flying into Vienna's Schwechat Airport then taking a one-hour minibus transfer or taxi ride along the 60km road just as convenient.

Some Slovak words to help you find your way around

ulica (street) This is usually omitted in both speaking and writing.
námestie (square) There are many of these in Bratislava, usually filled with trees and benches, often abbreviated to *nám*.
cesta (road)
most (bridge)
záhrada (garden)
sad (park)
pešia zóna (pedestrian zone)
les (forest)
veža (tower)
cintorín (cemetery)
mýto (toll gate)
schody (steps)
pošta (post office)

hlavná stanica (main railway station)
autobusová stanica (bus station)
Dunaj (the Danube River)

WHEN TO VISIT (AND WHY)

It's been 15 years since the Velvet Revolution, 13 years since Slovakia became independent and more than 18 months since the country joined the EU, and the youngest capital in the new Europe is one of the most progressive in central Europe. There's never been a better time to visit Bratislava.

It takes only two hours to fly there from London, while on the ground Bratislava is an hour from Vienna, two from Budapest and three from Prague. The 'little big city' is a strategic hot-spot with a leisure industry to match.

Spring and summer in Bratislava can be really gorgeous. In the height of summer, the river Danube moderates the heat and there are many green spaces such as Devín and the Kamzík Hills to escape to, countless lakes to cool off in, the nearest being Zlaté Piesky a tram-ride away, and scores of leafy squares.

At the end of April, out come all the terrace tables and chairs outside the pubs, restaurants and cafés, turning the Old Town into 'one big open-air café'.

The autumn colours are beautiful. There are many parks in town and it is warm enough to sit outside a café and contemplate the historic scenery. Winter is also atmospheric with the snow, the Christmas markets and the hills near by if you want to ski or hike.

Planning

Come in April and you'll probably have the place to yourself, apart from the occasional stag party (easily identified and avoided by their matching T-shirts proudly announcing 'Gary's Gang' or 'Plastered in Blava'), but the weather could be glorious. Personally, I got badly sunburnt in April, although the weather is as unpredictable as anywhere in Europe in the 21st century. Pack an anorak for occasional downpours, or secret trainspotting. Do bear in mind that some museums and castles such Devín are either closed during the winter or have a limited opening time.

Catch the butterfly
In June 2005, the Slovak Tourist Board announced its new marketing strategy. The aim was to present Slovakia as a young country with its own trademark and logo. The trademark was named 'Slovakia – Little Big Country' and incorporated a butterfly logo symbolising energy, life and colour. The main targets of the campaign are the Czech Republic, Poland and, surprisingly, the Netherlands. The Slovak Tourist Board (*www.cometoslovakia.com*) discovered that nature, hiking, historical landmarks and Bratislava are the biggest draws for tourists from these three countries.

HIGHLIGHTS/SUGGESTED ITINERARIES
Staying a weekend
- Walk along the Coronation route of Hungarian kings through the Old Town or if you're feeling lazy, sit on the tiny red tour 'train'

- Check out the history of the city in the Castle Museum and take in a breathless view from one of its towers. Sit out on the lawn and admire the view of the Danube and the postmodern concrete Petržalka housing estate, past the UFO café.
- Soak up the sun on a pavement terrace (café, bar, pub, restaurant)
- Walk up to the Slavín Monument for a panorama of the city
- Travel up the lift in the New Bridge to the UFO for a spectacular panoramic view
- Take the bus to Devín Castle for a Sunday afternoon stroll among the castle ruins and along the Danube and Morava riverbanks
- Work your way through half a dozen excellent local beers, finishing off with a shot of Borovička or Slivovica
- Try the Slovak national dish, Bryndzové halušky – gnocchi with sheep's cheese and bacon bits
- Take in a performance of world-class opera at spectacularly low prices; good seats for €5
- Visit the Blue Church, one of the most amazing churches in Europe, covered in blue icing

Staying a week or longer

- Take the trolleybus to Kamzík and after a tramp through the woods enjoy a slowly spinning view of Bratislava and its surroundings from the Veža restaurant or café at the top of the TV tower

NOT TO BE MISSED – THE TOP TEN

1 Opera at the SND
2 Castle
3 UFO café
4 Kamzík Veža revolving restaurant
5 Devín
6 Blue Church
7 Pálffy Palace and Mirbach Palace
8 St Martin's mini-cathedral
9 Michael's Tower view
10 Borovička & Bryndzové halušky

- Hire a canoe and paddle along the Danube
- Hire a bike and do one of the tours along the riverbank
- Travel the length of the Small Carpathian Wine Route, sampling along the way
- Visit the largest medieval cellars in central Europe at Červený Kameň
- Visit the Gabčikovo dam wildlife region
- Visit the Danubiana gallery at Čuňovo
- Take a boat trip to Vienna or Budapest

TOUR OPERATORS (WORLDWIDE)

Package holidays, city breaks, tailor-made tours and flights are readily available through UK- and US-based tour operators specialising in eastern Europe.

In addition to those below, see also *Local tours* and *Local travel agents* (pages 102–3), some of which can arrange accommodation etc.

In the UK

Archers Direct Booking hotline: 0870 460 3894; e mail@archersdirect.co.uk; www.archersdirect.co.uk. Offers coach trips to and around Slovakia, including escorted tours.

Cycle Riders Victoria Works, Lambridge Mews, Bath BA1 6QE; ↘ 01225 428452; www.biketours.co.uk. Organises a two-week tour cycling from Krakow to Budapest through central Slovakia, although it does not pass through Bratislava.

Jules Verne Tours 21 Dorset Sq, London NW1 6QG; ↘ 020 7616 1000; f 020 7723 8629; e sales@vjv.co.uk; www.vjv.co.uk. Trips include a three-night visit (from £285) to Bratislava, called rather irritatingly 'Prague's Other Half'. Also calls the Carlton 'five star' which is incorrect, although it deserves five-star rating.

Martin Randall Travel Voysey House, Barley Mow Passage, London W4 4GF; ↘ 020 8742 3355; f 020 8742 7766; e info@martinrandall.co.uk; www.martinrandall.com. Tours entitled Habsburg Empire, the Austro-Hungarian Music Festival and the Iron Curtain all include visits to Bratislava.

Operas Abroad The Tower, Mill Lane, Rainhill, Prescot, Merseyside L35 6NE; ↘/f 0151 493 0382; e info@operasabroad.com; www.operasabroad.com. Run by Regent Holidays (see next listing), this specialist tour operator arranges four-day tour packages to Budapest that feature three opera performances.

Regent Holidays 15 John St, Bristol BS1 2HR; ℡ 0117 921 1711; f 0117 925 4866; e regent@regent-holidays.co.uk; www.regent-holidays.co.uk. Independent operator specialising in eastern European destinations and offering a variety of itineraries.

Stag tours to eastern Europe

See also *Chapter 3* for many more stag-party organisers. 'Untouched', 'undiscovered', 'unspoilt' are all adjectives luring you to Slovakia for the pre-nuptial partying of your life. Here are some companies that probably hope you won't be 'untouched' and 'unspoilt':

Red Seven Leisure Kensington St, Brighton BN1 4AJ; ℡ 0870 751 7377; www.redsevenleisure.co.uk/destinations/Slovakia/Bratislava/stag.php

Big Weekends.com ℡ 0870 744 2251; www.bigweekends.com/bratislava.htm

http://www.travel-quest.co.uk/tqdance.htm Has endless stag possibilities.

http://www.lastnightoffreedom.co.uk/Abroad/abr_pac.htm 'For the more sophisticated stag…'

In the USA and Canada

E Tours European Walking Tours GmbH, 1401 Regency Dr East, Savoy, IL 61874; ℡ +1 866 443 8687 (toll-free), +1 217 398 0779; f +1 217 398 0484; www.etours.cz. Your incoming tour operator in Czech Republic and Slovakia, head office based in Prague.

Tour operators

Trip Central Tripcentral.ca, Lloyd D Jackson Sq, 2 King Street West, Hamilton, Ontario L8P 1A1; ☎ +1 800 665 4981 (in Canada and USA); e enquiry@tripcentral.ca; www.tripcentral.ca. The Bohemian tour takes in Budapest, Bratislava, Vienna and Prague.
Weber Travel Agency 3729 Grand Bd, Brookfield, IL 60513; ☎ +1 800 886 7012, +1 708 485 1333; f +1 708 485 5024; e travel@webertravel.com; www.webertravel.com. Puts together tours for individuals or groups to the Czech Republic and Slovakia. An eight-day tour of Slovakia (from US$2,575) explores hidden parts of the country.

In Australia
Intrepid Travel 360 Bourke St, Melbourne, Victoria 3000; ☎ +61 03 8602 0500; f +61 03 8602 0555; e info@intrepidtravel.com; www.intrepidtravel.com. Has many trips to central Europe, although there doesn't appear to be anything to Slovakia yet. Pester them.

Nature specialists
Sunbird PO Box 76, Sandy, Bedfordshire SG19 1DF; ☎ 01767 262522; f 01767 262916; e sunbird@sunbirdtours.co.uk; www.sunbirdtours.co.uk. A well-regarded birdwatching tour company that runs programmes in the Carpathian Mountains, for bird and bear watching. Twitchers can also do a combined Slovakia and Hungary trip.
The Travelling Naturalist e jamie@naturalist.co.uk; www.naturalist.co.uk. Organises a 'Birds and Bears' trip to Slovakia, mostly in the High Tatras, not including Bratislava.
Top Bicycle ☎ +420 519 513 745; f +420 519 513 746; e info@topbicycle.com; www.topbicycle.com/BicycleToursSlovakia.htm

Krakus (based in Krakow) Rynek Glowny 30, 31 010 Krakow, Poland; ☏ +48 12 432 3110;
f +48 12 421 3220; e michal@krakus.com.pl; www.krakus.com. A Polish company specialising
in business and leisure trips to Poland, Slovakia, Czech Republic, Hungary and Baltic States.

RED TAPE
Entry requirements
All visitors to Slovakia need a valid passport for the duration of stay in the country,
or if a visa is required visitors must present a passport with more than three
months left till the date of expiry. Citizens from EU member countries and
Switzerland can enter Slovakia with just a valid national identity card (where the
country concerned issues such cards).

British nationals may visit Slovakia with a valid passport for a period of up to 180
days, while the other EU countries' citizens may stay in the country for up to 90
days. Nationals from Australia, Canada, Israel, South Korea, Liechtenstein, Malaysia,
New Zealand, Andorra, Aruba and Chile may stay in Slovakia with a valid passport
for up to 90 days.

Nationals from Iceland, Monaco, Norway and Switzerland may stay for up to
three months and if this seems the same as 90 days, it is probably because most
passport and visa regulations are reciprocal and highly tit-for-tat, following each
detail to the last letter. Nationals from the USA along with Bulgaria, Croatia, Cuba,
Romania, San Marino, South Africa and Vatican City may stay for up to 30 days, while
nationals from Singapore and Hong Kong get up to only 14 days.

Red tape

Nationals from all other countries require a visa and should contact the Embassy of the Slovak Republic in their home country before setting off. Slovak embassies and consulates abroad are listed on page 66.

The list on the website at www.foreign.gov.sk/En/index.html (then click on 'visa requirements') gives an updated list of all mutual, unilateral and partial visa agreements.

Visitors to Slovakia wishing to extend their stay should apply for a visa at the Slovak embassy in their home country before setting out and allow four weeks for processing. For visas you will need two recent passport photos. As a guideline for visa prices, in the US a single-entry visa costs US$51, a double-entry US$63 and multiple- entry US$126.

For US citizens on private, tourist, official or business visits, a Slovak visa is not required for stays up to 90 days, but a passport valid for at least three months after the last intended day of stay in Slovakia is required. A child younger than five years of age may be included in a parent's passport.

Foreigners who intend to work, study, teach or work in Slovakia may apply for a temporary stay permit at a Slovak embassy or consulate general in their home country.

According to a new Slovak law, the border police have the right to request proof of a medical insurance policy covering all hospitalisation and medical treatment costs in Slovakia. Travellers should therefore make certain they have medical cover before setting off.

The border police also have the right to request evidence that you can afford to stay in Slovakia spending the equivalent of US$60 per person per day. Foreigners can demonstrate sufficient funds by means of cash or a statement from a bank account accessible in Slovakia, but bank debit and credit cards are not accepted, unless there is an ATM machine at the border and a statement can be shown immediately. Do not worry too much about these terrifying-sounding regulations; they are imposed very rarely.

Police registration

If you plan to stay in Slovakia on a long-term basis, ie: to work or live, you must register with the police within three days of arrival. You will need your passport and proof of accommodation. It appears to have been abolished for tourists, although there are reports of officious hotel receptionists. City Hotel Bratislava seems quite keen on forms.

Customs regulations

Travellers over 16 can take 200 cigarettes, 100 cigarillos, 50 cigars or 250g of tobacco (or a combination of the respective amounts), 250ml of cologne and 50g of perfume in and out of Slovakia. As for alcohol, you can carry in one litre of spirits or two litres of wine, but you'll find much better prices in the Bratislava supermarkets so why bother lugging over a load of bottles. Save your energy for picking up a nice bottle of Borovička to take home and tempt your maiden aunts. A maximum of ten litres of petrol can be carried in canisters for emergency use and presents and other items up to the value of €175 can be brought in and taken out of the country. Pets can be transported only with all the necessary pet passports and vaccination certificates. Antiques and works of art require a licence and are subject to customs duty.

SLOVAK EMBASSIES OVERSEAS

Australia 47 Culgoa Circuit, O' Malley OBEO, Canberra, ACT 2606; ℩ +612 6290 1516; f +612 6290 1755; e slovak@cyberone.com.au; www.slovakemb-aust.org

Austria Armbrustergasse 24, A-1190 Vienna; ℩ +43 1 318 9055 200; f +43 1 318 9055 208; e zuwien@aon.at; www.slovak-trade.at

Canada 50 Rideau Terrace, Ottawa, Ontario K1M 2A1; ℩ +1 613 749 4442: f +1 613 749 4989; e slovakemb@sprlnt.ca; www.ottawa.mfa.sk

Czech Republic Pod Hradbami 1, 160 00 Prague 6; ℩ +42 2 3332 1441; f +42 2 3332 4289; e skembassy@pha.inecnet.cz; www.prague.mfa.sk

France 125, rue du Ranelagh, 750 16 Paris; ℩ +33 1 44 14 51 22; f +33 1 42 88 76 53; e paris@amb-slovaquie.fr; www.paris.mfa.sk

Germany Pariser Strasse 44, 107 07 Berlin; ℩ +49 30 88 92 620; f +49 30 88 92 6222; e presse@botschaft-slowakei.de; www.botschaft-slowakei.de

Hungary Stefánia út 22–24, 1143 Budapest; ℩ +36 1 460 9010; f +36 1 460 9020; e slovakem@matavnet.hu; www.budapest.mfa.sk

Irish Republic 20 Clyde Rd, Ballsbridge, Dublin 4: ℩ +353 1 6600 012; f +353 1 6600 014; e slovak@iol.ie; www.dublin.mfa.sk

Italy Via dei Prati della Farnesina 57, 00194 Rome; ☏ +39 6 332 70061; e amb.slovac@tin.it; www.roma.mfa.sk

Poland ul. Litewska 6, 00-581 Warsaw; ☏ +48 22 5258 110; f +48 22 5258 122; e slovakia@waw.pdi.net; www.amasada-slowacji.pdi.pl

Russia ul J Fucíka 17–19, Moscow; ☏ +70 95 956 4920; f +70 95 250 1591; e skem@col.ru; www.moscow.mfa.sk

South Africa 930 Arcadia St, Arcadia, Pretoria; ☏ +27 12 3422 051; f +27 12 3423 688; e slovakem@mweb.co.za; www.pretoria.mfa.sk

United Kingdom 25 Kensington Palace Gardens, London W8 4QY; ☏ +44 207 313 6470; f +44 207 313 6481; e mail@slovakembassy.co.uk; www.slovakembassy.co.uk

USA 3523 International Court, NW, Washington, DC 20008; ☏ +1 202 237 1054; f +1 202 237 6438; e info@slovakembassy-us.org; www.slovakembassy-us.org

GETTING THERE
By air

Travellers to Bratislava are lucky as they have two options of airport – Bratislava and Vienna airport (only 60km away) – giving more variety of route, cost, timing and budget flight options. Ticket prices to Bratislava/Vienna will be higher during peak summer season (June–August) and at Christmas and New Year.

Discount travel websites such as www.cheapflights.co.uk, www.expedia.com and www.lastminute.co.uk can offer bargain flights.

From the UK
Direct flights to Bratislava M R Štefánik Airport
Bratislava Airport (M R Štefánik) is 9–12km (5–7 miles) from the city centre. Buses run to the city (travel time 30 minutes). Taxis are also available (travel time 20 minutes): www.letiskobratislava.sk

AirSlovakia ❯ 02 4342 2744; www.airslovakia.sk. Flies to Bratislava from Birmingham using a Boeing 757.
Czech Airlines Štúrova 13; ❯ 02 5296 1325; f 02 5296 1070; e bts@czechairlines.com; www.csa.cz, www.czechairlines.com. Flies London to Bratislava via Prague.
easyJet ❯ 0870 600 0000; www.easyjet.com. Popular low-cost airline. Flights daily from Luton direct to Bratislava from £41 (inc taxes). Easy-to-use booking system and useful for people from London and the Midlands; they also fly to Vienna.
Lufthansa www.lufthansa.co.uk. Has some special deals on flights to Bratislava. Comfortable airline which flies daily from London Heathrow, Manchester, Edinburgh and Birmingham.
Ryanair www.ryanair.com. Flies London Stansted to Bratislava twice daily; prices from £5.99 (not inc taxes). This new route began 30 Oct 2005.
Sky Europe ❯ 020 7365 0365; www.skyeurope.com. The Slovak budget airline flies between London Stansted and Bratislava and also Manchester and Bratislava.

From the Irish Republic
SkyEurope flights from Dublin to Bratislava with very reasonable prices.

From the US and the rest of the world
There are no direct flights from the US to Bratislava; instead fly to Amsterdam/London/Frankfurt then get a low-cost flight to Bratislava. Or fly to Vienna then go by land (shuttle bus) to Bratislava.

Airport transfer from Bratislava Airport into the centre
Airport transfer is operated non-stop by Hunter Slovakia; ☎ 02 4364 3033 or 0904 977 907 & 0908 977 907 (both cell phones); www.airportshuttle.sk. You can also pre-book your door-to-door transfer online with easyJet's transfer partner A-T-S. From Bratislava to the city centre and Vienna, easyJet's transfer partner operates a private taxi service.

   Alternatively, you can take bus 61 from the airport to the main railway station (*hlavá stanica*) then tram 1 into the centre. This will take 30–40 minutes and you'll need to buy tickets (*lístky*) at the airport.

Taxi There is a taxi rank in front of the terminal building. Taxis take 20 minutes from the centre. Expect to pay 300–600Sk.

Car hire For special easyJet inflight rates visit the Europcar desk on arrival; ☎ +386 206 1684.

Direct flights to Vienna Schwechat International Airport
Vienna International Airport (Schwechat) is 64km from Bratislava and can be used as a gateway for intercontinental travellers. www.viennaairport.com.

Getting there

Air Berlin www.airberlin.com. Offer some very cheap tickets into Vienna from London Stansted. Once in Vienna take a shuttle transfer to Bratislava.

Austrian Airlines ☏ 020 7434 7350; www.aua.com. Fly from London Gatwick to Vienna four times a day; prices from £70 return. The Austrian Airlines Group owns 62% per Slovak Airlines, and will revitalise schedules from Bratislava.

Vienna Airport details and transfer to Bratislava

Flying to Vienna Schwechat Airport and then taking the 64km bus/shuttle/taxi ride to Bratislava greatly increases your options of when and how to travel to and from Bratislava. There are more flights (including budget), a greater range of airlines and a great choice of when you fly (so you don't have to get up at 04.00, as with some low-cost flights). The trip from the airport usually takes under an hour, although border crossing delays may add some time.

SkyEurope www.skyeurope.com. New bus shuttle service between Vienna's city centre and Bratislava Airport.

Slovakia Green Tours www.slovakiagreentours.com. Also offer a shuttle and limousine service from Schwechat Airport to Bratislava.

By train

If you don't fancy flying, or want to stop off en route, try the train. First cross the Channel by Eurostar (*www.eurostar.com*). Slovak railways (*www.zsr.sk*) has information in English about train connections. You'll arrive at Bratislava's main railway station, *hlavná stanica*, a bustling centre of life. From here, tram 1 takes you straight into town, or there are banks of taxis who'll do the same for a reasonable 300Sk. If worried about Bratislava cabbies' undeserved bad reputation, ask about the price first, but you'll probably hurt his feelings and he'll point tearfully to the meter.

The most convenient route to the Slovak Republic from western Europe is via Vienna or Prague.

Rail passes

Interrail (*www.interrail.com*) divides Europe up into a number of zones. Slovakia is in zone D. Passes for adults (over 26) cost from £215 (for 16 days' travel in Zone D: Slovakia, Czech Republic, Hungary, Poland, Croatia, Bosnia) to £405 for one month's journey around a possible 28 European countries. Under-26 year olds can get a youth ticket costing £145–285 for the same parameters. Remember that an interrail pass is not valid in the holder's country of residence.

Passes can be bought from the Rail Europe Travel Centre (*178 Piccadilly, London W1*; ✆ *0870 830 2000*; e *reservations@raileurope.co.uk; www.raileurope.co.uk*).

You cannot buy a London–Bratislava train ticket online because it involves more than three changes. It's really better to go by air.

Slovak State Railways (ŽSR or Železnice Slovenskej Republiky) www.zsr.sk/english

By coach

Check out Eurolines (*www.eurolines.co.uk or www.nationalexpress.co.uk*) although the 30½-hour journey is totally exhausting and unlikely to be cheaper than a budget flight. Two companies manage Coach Line Bratislava–Vienna: SkyEurope Airlines and Eurolines.

The Slovak national bus company (*www.sad.sk*) is abbreviated rather mournfully, as SAD or Slovenská autobusová doprava.

Bratislava bus station Mlynské nivy 21
Eurolines Bus station; ☏ 02 5542 4870

By car

You need motorway stickers for toll payments. See www.viamichelin.co.uk for details of routes

It is about 1,500km by road from London to Bratislava and the journey would take more than 18 hours. The route, once on the continent, goes via Dunkerque, Brussels, Leuven, Aachen, Cologne, Frankfurt and Linz.

Traffic regulations

The road signs correspond to European norms. The speed limit in the cities and villages is 60km/h, outside the cities and villages 90km/h, and on highways 130km/h. Safety belts must also be used in cities. Drivers are strictly prohibited from drinking alcohol.

Car rental
See *Chapter 4*, page 109.

By hydrofoil
Down the Danube from Vienna, upstream from Budapest (*www.lod.sk*). From Budapest check out www.mahartpassnave.hu. International connections from Austria and Hungary are possible on the Danube which is also linked with the Rhine, the Black Sea and the Main.

HEALTH
The standard of public health in Slovakia is very good. The tap water is potable and safe, and even has a fairly palatable taste. However, cheap and beneficial mineral water is also available in shops, cafés, restaurants and hotel minibars (10–15Sk for a 1.5 litre bottle).

No vaccinations are legally required but it is wise to be up to date with routine vaccinations such as **diphtheria**, **tetanus** and **polio**. **Hepatitis A** should also be considered. For those who are going to be working in hospitals or in close contact with children, **hepatitis B** vaccination is recommended. Rabid deer and foxes roam the Slovak countryside so pre-exposure rabies vaccine (ideally three doses given over a minimum of 21 days) should also be considered for anyone who is going to be working with animals.

The sun is very strong in central Europe. Take a supply of suntan lotion and after-sun care, or look in the local shopping mall. The air content is relatively good as there is not so much industry in Slovakia; however, almost everybody smokes heavily.

The **cuisine** is very heavy on the meat and fat, and locals have already joined the world trend towards obesity. Cases of bovine spongiform encephalopathy (mad cow disease) have been reported in cattle in Slovakia. To avoid risk don't try the often-offered beef tartare which involves raw meat spread on toast. Alcoholism is not as widespread as in neighbouring countries, but with the availability of powerful, cheap spirits, it's sensible to watch your intake.

People don't **swim** in the Danube because of the strong current and pollution, but there are many local lakes where the water is pretty clean (Zlaté Piesky, Senec, Ružinov). **Mosquitoes** are irritating and the Danube in summer is plagued by the little devils. If you stay on one of the three botels (hotels on a boat), take a good supply of insect repellent and cream.

If you intend to go **walking** or **cycling** in the countryside remember that a tick bite can cause the potentially deadly disease **encephalitis**. The TBE- (tick-borne encephalitis) infected tick population is now endemic in 16 European countries, including Slovakia, Austria and Hungary. Vaccination against tick-borne encephalitis may be available in the UK (on a named patient basis) and comprises a series of three injections that can be done over three to four weeks. Take advice from your doctor or a reputable travel clinic. Whether you are immunised or not you should make sure that you wear suitable clothing, such as long trousers tucked into boots, and a hat. Also use tick repellents and at the end of the walk check yourself for ticks or better still get someone to do it for you. If you are travelling with young children you need to be especially careful to check their hair as ticks have a habit of dropping from overhanging branches. If you discover a tick then it is important to remove it slowly and carefully to avoid damaging the mouthpiece. Use tweezers or failing that your thumb and forefinger wrapped in tissue paper. Medical advice should be sought locally, as treatment following exposure may be available. Tell the doctor whether or not you have been immunised. Tick alert 2005 (*www.masta.org/tickalert*) has more information.

For **emergency telephone numbers**, see page 96.

Health insurance

Slovakia has one of the cheapest and most professional health services in the world. Tourists with health insurance will be well cared for and those from EU countries need to carry an electronic card (European Health Insurance Card [EHIC]) which replaced the E111 form guaranteeing free health care. Everyone travelling to Slovakia should take out travel insurance, even for a short weekend break.

Visit the Department of Health website at www.dh.gov.uk/PolicyAndGuidance/HealthAdviceForTravellers/fs/en.

The UK Foreign & Commonwealth Office has a website for its 'Know Before You Go' campaign, giving advice on all aspects of travel, at www.fco.gov.uk/health.

Health

Travel clinics and health information

A full list of current travel clinic websites worldwide is available on www.istm.org. For other journey preparation information, consult www.tripprep.com (registration needed). Information about symptoms and medication can be found on www.emedicine.com/wild/topiclist.htm.

Pharmacies

For minor ailments, a visit to the nearest pharmacy (*lekáreň*) may suffice. There are many in Bratislava, some opening until late and some offering a 24-hour emergency service.

Lekáreň Novafarm Námestie SNP 20. Open Mon–Fri 08.00–19.00, Sat 08.00–17.00, Sun 09.00–17.00; also has 24-hour emergency service.

Lekáreň Pokrok Račianske mýto 1/A. Open Mon–Sat from 06.30–17.00; also has 24-hour emergency service.

Lekáreň Apotheke Samarítán Panská 13

Lekáreň u Zlatého Grífa Sedlárska 2. Look for the golden griffin hanging above the door.

Hospitals

In emergencies **Acad L Dérer's Faculty Hospital** has a clinic, Kramáre, at Limbová ulica 3; ☏ 02 5954 1111.

Faculty Hospital Ružinvoská ulica 10; ☏ 02 4433 2409

Dentist
English-speaking dentist Dr Mamoun Al-Zafari, Lazaretská ulica 35; ☎ 02 5292 7729.

Alcoholics Anonymous
An English-speaking group meets every Sunday at 19.00 at Zrinského 2, situated in the hilly residential area of Bratislava, just beyond the churchyard on Palisády. Take bus 208 to the end stop. For more information e aabrat@pobox.sk.

Spas
Slovaks are also wildly enthusiastic about the curative powers of spa waters. The nearest spa to Bratislava is at Piešťany, where the waters are particularly soothing for bones and joints. Piešťany is only 80km from Bratislava, so you could combine a holiday with a water cure and go home not only refreshed but regenerated.

Piešťany is one of the most popular European health spas and the most important in Slovakia. Its reputation is based on the healing powers of the thermal waters, sulphurous mud and excellent medical care. Piešťany waters are famous for treating locomotor disorders, rheumatologic and neurological problems and it provides excellent therapy after injuries or orthopaedic surgery.

The resort has dozens of hotels, but the best is probably the Balnea Esplanade (part of the Danubius Hotel Group), Winterova 29, 921 29 Piešťany; ☎ +421 33 775 77 33; f +421 33 775 77 39; e reservations@healthspa.sk; www.spa-piestany.sk.

SAFETY
Crime

Bratislava is a safe city for travellers, with a low rate of violent crime. There is, however, a high incidence of petty theft. Pickpockets operate around the main tourist areas, the railway station and in large shopping malls and foreigners are easily identified and targeted. Cameras, mobile phones and small electrical items (computers, games etc) are as attractive as cash and credit cards. Take sensible precautions against bag-snatching and mugging. Do not leave valuables unattended or anything on show in a hire car.

You will see many homeless people in Bratislava, sitting outside Tesco, on Námestie SNP and on Hviezdoslavovo námestie. They are harmless, drinking cheap wine and look too tired to hassle tourists although I saw one tall homeless man picking on a little Roma lad who always stands outside McDonald's. He was threatening him in a particularly unpleasant manner.

You must carry your passport with you at all times as identification. Keep it safe, in a zipped-up pocket or secure bag and keep a photocopy of the details separately in case you do lose it. Contact your embassy in Bratislava immediately if you do lose your passport; the embassy contact list is on pages 98–100.

Check restaurant bills; restaurants are legally required to provide a receipt from the electronic till. Taxi drivers have an undeserved reputation for ripping off foreigners. I took countless taxis in Bratislava and without exception they were inexpensive and the drivers courteous and charming.

Taking photographs of anything that could be perceived as a military establishment or somehow of security interest, may result in problems with the authorities.

When driving, remember there is a zero tolerance of alcohol and hand-held mobile phone use when driving is also illegal. There are spot fines for speeding or drinking.

When walking around at night, avoid the stations or deserted parts of town. Travellers with darker skin colour should be aware that there is a nasty rash of nationalist skinheads in parts of Slovakia. They tend to be spotty nerds who focus on what they see as historical injustices but would not be pleasant to encounter in a dark alley.

For emergency telephone numbers see page 96.

Women on their own

Slovak men are courteous, if a little old-fashioned regarding women. Feminism is still a new concept and women on their own are more pitied than pestered.

Police

In Slovakia, the police are badly paid and susceptible to bribes. They will often set up road checks and often target cars with a foreign number plate. Foreigners are allowed to drive in Slovakia as long as they have a valid licence from their home country and have been in Slovakia for less than 30 days. If you have been speeding or have committed a traffic infraction, the police can fine you up to 500Sk on the spot, or take you to the station and fine you up to 2,000Sk. Ask for a receipt for the fine; if nothing appears, ask for the policeman's badge number. If you intend to stay in Slovakia for more than 30 days, you must hold an international driver's licence valid for Europe.

Terrorism

There is continuous police presence outside the US Embassy on Hviezdoslavovo námestie, next to the Radisson SAS Carlton Hotel. This has been in operation since the Bush–Putin summit in Bratislava (February 2005) when security was stepped up but fortunately these are the only signs a visitor will see. You will only undergo a security check when entering certain government offices, airports and embassies.

There have been no terrorist attacks in Slovakia. Slovakia is a very small player on the international scene and there are no cities with more than 500,000 inhabitants. Nevertheless the threat of terrorism is taken seriously and all necessary preventive measures are in place. On 11 June 2005, Reuters reported that a suicide bomber blew himself up outside the Slovak Embassy in Baghdad; he was reportedly targeting a meeting of agents of the US Central Intelligence Agency at the embassy. As a member of NATO and the allied coalition, Slovakia has sent troops to Iraq and Afghanistan.

The Wild East

There have been some spectacular Mafia killings in recent years, including the murders of two major city bosses, Jozef Svoboda and Peter Congrady, who were cut down in 2004. In 1997, an assassin scaled the roof of a Bratislava hospital to machine gun a patient, the same underworld boss he had earlier shot but failed to kill in an attack at a hotel.

In December 2004, a Bratislava restaurant was badly damaged by a bomb blast in which three Slovaks were injured. Local police attributed the bombing to warring Mafia factions and the restaurant was not in a tourist area. In a second incident in December 2004, a plastic bag containing an explosive device, which did not go off, was found in the Slavín residential area of Bratislava, about 200m from the villa of the Slovak president. Local authorities described the incident as criminal – not terrorist-related.

WHAT TO TAKE

Back in the bad old days, visitors to the Wild East had to pack a squash ball in with their toiletries to plug up the gaping hole in the bathroom sink. Fortunately such brutalities are a thing of the past. The two-pin electrical plugs are still problematic, but you can find adaptors plus everything and anything else you might need in Bratislava.

Stag-party travellers should pack some sportswear and a swimsuit as there's a huge variety of events on offer. A swimming costume is a good idea for all visitors, as Bratislava is surrounded by plenty of natural bathing possibilities; the lakes and the Small Danube are delightful destinations.

Bratislava is best explored on foot, so pack some comfortable shoes and perhaps an anorak for the occasional, unexpected summer shower. Winters can be chilly and summers stifling so choose clothes accordingly.

There are no restaurants that require a dinner jacket, but some casinos and nightclubs require a certain degree of smartness.

Take out comprehensive travel insurance before your trip to cover lost baggage, theft and medical emergencies, and bring copies of the documentation with you.

Bear in mind that Slovakia along with big sister the Czech Republic is famous for brewing some of the best beer in the world. The wines and spirits also merit serious investigation. Slovak cuisine is hearty and rib-sticking. Bearing all these factors in mind, it might be a good idea to pack extra supplies of headache and indigestion tablets.

ELECTRICITY

Slovakia's electrical current is 220 Volts/50Hz, accessible via the European two-pin plug. Plug adaptors for use with three-pronged plugs are generally available from large supermarkets and chemists in the city.

MONEY AND BUDGETING
Slovak money

After the split of Czechoslovakia in 1993, the National Bank of Slovakia introduced new banknotes and coins in 1993.

Slovakia's basic currency unit is the crown (koruna), with smaller sums denominated in haliers (halier). Coins come in denominations of 1, 2, 5 and 10 koruna and now only 50 halier; bills in denominations of 20, 50, 100, 200, 500, 1,000 and 5,000 koruna. **One koruna** equals 100 halier (haliers are of very little value and not used much anymore; the 50h piece is the only legal tender).

Coins
All have 'Slovenska Republika' and the Slovak Republic's coat of arms on the obverse.

10 halier Not legal tender from 1 Jan 2004; aluminium, showed 19th-century wooden belfry from Zemplin region.

20 halier Not legal tender from 1 Jan 2004; showed the peak of Kriváň in the Malá Fatra National Park.

50 halier Two versions! The 1996 issue is a tiny brown copper coin featuring Devín Castle and '50h' message. The 1993 issue is light-grey aluminium with Devín Castle – a bigger coin, the same size as the 2 koruna, but much cheaper metal.

1 koruna A goldish copper coin showing Gothic wooden statue of Madonna and Child from the 16th century.

2 koruna A silver coin with seated armless Venus statuette from 4000BC.

5 koruna A silver coin featuring an ancient Biatec Celtic coin from 100BC showing a horserider.

10 koruna A goldish large copper coin showing decorated cross cast in bronze from the 10th century AD.

Paper money

The front shows a figure from Slovak history, the reverse a historic church, castle or building in Slovakia.

20 koruna A light- and dark-green note with face in profile of Duke Pribina (9th century); reverse shows Nitra Castle.

50 koruna A light- and dark-blue note with faces of Saints Cyril and Methodius (linguistic missionaries to the Slavs in the 9th century); reverse shows hands with the old Slavonic alphabet 'hlaholika' and a medieval church near Nitra.

100 koruna An orangey-grey note with the face of Madonna, a woodcarving by Master Pavol of Levoča; reverse shows the church of St Jacob and the Town Hall in Levoča.

200 koruna A greeny-blue note with the face of Anton Bernolák (18–19th-century linguist); reverse shows Trnava, the city of churches.

500 koruna An orangey-blue note with face of Ľudovít Štúr, codifier of the Slovak language in the 19th century; reverse shows Bratislava Castle.

1,000 koruna A light-purple note with face of Monsigneur Andrej Hlinka, priest and politician (19–20th century) who is considered by many a heroic Slovak patriot as he was the leading advocate for Slovak independence between the wars. He was a reputed humanitarian, but some consider him a strident nationalist, fascist even. Reverse side shows the Madonna and the church of St Andrew in Ružomberok.

5,000 koruna An orangey-brown note shows Milan Rastislav Štefánik, astronomer, diplomat and war leader (19–20th century); reverse shows M R Štefánik's last resting place on Bradlo Hill.

The Slovak Republic is a member of the European Union (1 May 2004) but not yet in the Schengen Visa System (due 2007) or Euro Monetary System (due 2008). However, many top restaurants and hotels accept the euro and often list their prices in euros, while referring back to the base unit of Slovak koruna. The current **exchange rate** (October 2005) is £1 = 57Sk, US$1 = 32Sk, €1 = 39Sk.

For information on banks, exchanging currency, ATMs and travellers' cheques, see pages 88–90.

Budgeting

You can still find great bargains in Bratislava, although it is more expensive than the rest of the country. However, you can also go to the other end of the scale and have a right royal blow-out. Everyone will find something in the 'little big city' to suit their taste and purse and your money will go further in shops, restaurants, hotels and on public transport than in the West. The following guide lists daily budgets for one person, based on two people sharing accommodation (and therefore paying slightly less on the room, but not the beer bill...).

Penny-pinching You can probably get by on a budget of around 900Sk (€23/£15/US$28) for a hostel dorm, eating in one of the self-service canteens (*jedaleň*), entry to a few museums and rounded off by a meal in a modest restaurant.

Modest You'll spend about 1,500Sk (€39/£26/US$46) a day for basic accommodation in a two-star hotel, cheered on by occasional treats; the cheapest opera tickets are from 380Sk/€10 although you can get last-minute tickets for as little as €2.

Comfortable A daily allowance of 3,500Sk (€89/£60/US$107) will allow a stay in a three-star hotel, some sightseeing, stops for coffee, cake and beer, a meal in a decent restaurant, late-night drinks in a club and a taxi back to base.

Luxurious On a daily stipend of 6,000Sk (€154/£104/US$184) you can stay in one of the top four-star hotels in the centre, drink cocktails, eat like a lord, purchase some Modra ceramics, wind down by taking a taxi up to Kamzík Hill and sip cocktails in the Veža revolving tower, then back to town to a swish restaurant and on to a jazz club for some chill-out sounds.

Splurging The wallet could be as much as 10,000Sk (€257/£174/US$306) a day lighter if you're going to go berserk and Bratislava's a good place to do it. Book into one of the top trio of hotels, take your pick from the designer shops along Michalska and Ventúrska, take a trip out to the Small Carpathian Wine Route, dine out at Le Monde and splash out on more vintage white wines, including a Slovak version of Tokay. Get the best seats in the house at the opera and then gamble what's left in your pocket at one of the four classy casinos.

Tipping

Tipping is standard practice in restaurants, cafés, bars and pubs. It is called *prepitné* (for a drink) in Slovak. To calculate a tip it is best to round the figure to the nearest 10Sk. However, if two beers came to 58Sk, giving 60Sk is a bit mean when it's just over two euros, so round it up to 70Sk. The standard rate is around 10–15%. In taxis, round the figure up to the nearest 50Sk or 100Sk (if it's over 50Sk) or calculate 10–15%. Saying *d'akujem* (thank you) when you hand over any money is a good way of adding in the tip but must be done with extreme care as it means 'I don't want any change back, thank you'.

Some say tipping is not required, but a 10% rule is slowly taking hold in Slovakia. Still, if you did not like the service, you can refuse to leave any tip. Leaving tips does not mean leaving the money on the table and simply departing. In fact, when the waiter brings the bill, he/she waits till you pay. When paying, tell the waiter the total sum (the payment plus the tip). Therefore, it is a common practice simply to round up the bill to the nearest tens or hundreds and not to bother with the exact tip calculation.

Money and budgeting

Practicalities

BANKS

Banking services are provided in Bratislava by both Slovak and foreign banks. Inside banks visitors can use the exchange offices during office hours (Monday–Thursday 08.00–17.00, Friday 08.00–15.00) and ATM machines on the outer walls or within a secure room reached with a swipe card. The most frequently accepted credit cards are MasterCard and Visa.

Businesses are usually open Monday–Friday 09.00–17.00. Shops are open 08.00–18.00; supermarkets and chain stores 08.00–20.00. Shops close at noon on Saturday, and some chain stores are open on Sunday. The website www.banky.sk gives advice on Slovak banks.

Slovak National Bank Sturova 2; ☎ 07 323 511; f 07 364-721

ČSOB (Ceskoslovenska obchodni banka a.s. pobocka). Open Mon–Thu 08.00–17.00, Fri 08.00–16.00.

TB (Tatra Banka) ☎ 02 5919 1000; www.tatrabanka.sk. Has a list of ATMs and where to find them (including Visa).

Exchanging currency

There are many bureaux de change booths in the Old Town.

You can buy Slovak koruna in banks (see above). Hotels can also give somewhat higher rates outside banking hours. Visitors arriving at the main railway station are immediately warned 'Do not change money in the street', but there's no need to invest in the dodgy-looking fellow with a wad of zlotys; there are dozens of zmenáreň (currency-exchange offices) all over town. In Bratislava, there is an exchange office on Rybárska brána near Hviezdoslavovo námestie that is open until 20.00. More exchange offices can be found along Michalská/Ventúrska.

Some hotels and exchange offices in the city centre offer exchange facilities at the weekend. Many of the top hotels and restaurants now accept payment in euros.

Travellers' cheques
Travellers' cheques are the safest way to carry money but make sure that you buy them from an organisation with agents in Slovakia. Change cash and travellers' cheques at proper banks or bureaux de change as kiosks offer poor exchange rates. If your money is lost or stolen you can arrange for friends or relatives in the UK to transfer money through Western Union to the Tatra Banka. Call Western Union in the UK on 0800 833 833 for information. International accounts can be drawn from an ATM, usually marked Bankomat.

Visa TravelMoney
Visa TravelMoney Travelex (✆ 020 7837 9580; e customerservices@travelex.com) is a convenient, safe alternative to carrying piles of cash or cheques. The system is based on a pre-paid travel card that allows holders 24-hour access to their money in any local currency. You load up the card with funds before your trip and draw the cash

Banks

out from ATM machines as you go along. When you've used up your funds simply throw the card away.

Credit cards

Major credit cards (American Express, Diners Club, Visa and MasterCard/Eurocard) and debit cards (Maestro and Visa Electron) may be used to withdraw cash from ATMs of major banks (VÚB, Tatra Banka, Slovenská Sporitelna) and for payments in larger hotels, restaurants, shops and petrol stations. Smaller shops, museums and ticket offices may be reluctant to accept credit cards, so keep some koruna handy.

MEDIA
Print

The Slovak press is independent (foreign and locally owned) and suffers from hangovers of the past suffocating regime combined with an excess of magazines. Thousands of trees have been pulped to produce the vast range of magazines on every subject under the sun, but particularly lifestyle and women's magazines. *Kam do Mesta* (Where to go in Town) is a handy pocket-sized free listings guide. It comes out once a month and you can get copies in the BKIS office at Klobučnícka 2. It is all in Slovak but the information on bars, concerts, films etc is quite easy to decipher. The times are given in the 24-hour clock. The first page lists all the name days for that month, so you won't miss an opportunity to wish the beautiful Angela

(11 March) who just brought you a cool beer a happy name day (*želám krásne meniny!*). There is also an online version at www.kamdomesta.sk.

Nový čas (New Time) is the best-selling Slovak daily tabloid, published by Ringier Slovakia, a subsidiary of the Swiss Ringier company; www.novycas.sk.

Život (Life) a weekly, *Nový čas pre ženy* (New Time for Women), *Eurotelevízia* and *Telemagazín* and the monthlies *Eva* and *Rebecca* are all published by Ringier Slovakia; www.bleskovky.sk.

The Slovak daily *Pravda* (Truth) is a colour tabloid and available free if you are walking around the Old Town as there is always a teenager handing out complimentary copies. Or you can buy it in the newsagents for 10Sk. One of its supplements is *Moment* (*www.moment.sk*) formerly a loss-making TV listings magazine now incorporated into *Pravda* and published every Thursday. *Pravda* is second in popularity behind *Nový čas* and has a good online edition at www.pravda.sk.

Týžden (Week) is the newest weekly on the stands, with one-third owned by entrepreneur Ladislav Rehák, formerly involved with the radio station Radio Expres.

Sme (*www.sme.sk*) is a daily paper and flagship of Petit Press, Alaxej Fulmek's group, backed by the German Veragsgruppe Passau company. *Sme* used to wage war against the Mečiar government, now it is more moderate and tends to back the right wing of the governing coalition.

Plus 7 dní (Plus 7 days) is the greatest success of the 7 Plus group, formed by three Slovak partners. Other titles published by the 7 Plus group include *Šarm* (Charm) and *Báječna žena* (Wonderful Woman).

The Slovak news agency, **Tasr**, has an English-language page on its website at www.tasr.sk/indeng.php.

English-language press

The **Slovak Spectator** is a weekly newspaper published on Mondays with news, features, arts and sports. The *Spectator* also publishes a large number of off-shoots: **Spex** (40Sk), a monthly glossy magazine with features and entertainment listings; **Spectacular Slovakia** (165Sk), annual magazine; the annual **Book of Lists** (149Sk); an annual magazine entitled **Career and Employment Guide** (89Sk); and an annual **Real Estate and Construction Guide** (89Sk). If that weren't enough to keep you occupied, there's also an annual **Investment Advisory Guide** (89Sk) if you like what you see in Bratislava and plan on investing in the region. The *Slovak Spectator* costs 40Sk although you can pick up a complimentary copy in most hotel foyers. The online edition can be found at www.slovakspectator.sk, although registration is now required.

Business Slovakia, published by *Bratislava Business Journal* and editor-in-chief Ian Brodie, is a tabloid-sized bi-monthly with only 12 shiny pages. The magazine sells for 40Sk and their offices are on a steep street leading up to the castle at Zámocké schody 4 (℡ 02 5464 1471; e businessslovakia@stonline.sk).

The *BBJ* offer a range of business services, from translating and interpreting to advice on setting up businesses in Slovakia and real-estate searches (e bbj@stonline.sk). The company is also connected to the Castle Club who rent out apartments for short-term residential or business clients (see *Accommodation* on pages 138–9).

Just to confuse us all there is another similarly named publication in this modest-sized business community, **Business Journal Slovakia**. This monthly glossy A4-sized publication costs 59Sk and comes from another British gentleman, James Mackintosh (✆ *02 5443 1467;* e *editor@bjs.sk*). The full text of the *BJS* is available at www.bjs.sk.

What's On Bratislava & Slovakia is a bilingual lifestyle and cultural magazine, selling for 40Sk and also from the stables of Mr Mackintosh. The print version is more helpful than that online at www.whatsonslovakia.com.

Television

The TV networks (*televízne siete*) you can watch in Slovakia with only an aerial are the three basic terrestrial Slovak ones.

State TV channels **STV1** and **STV2** (*www.stv.sk*) managed to boost their ratings recently by showing **Superstar**, a talent contest for singers along the lines of *Pop Idol*. The nation was gripped in the spring of last year by the last three left from a starting line-up that featured a 19-year-old lad from Žilina, Tomáš Bezdeda, who looked like a young Brad Pitt, and two disarmingly modest young ladies, 16-year-old Martina Šindlerová who was accompanied everywhere by her dad and Katarína Koščová, 23, who eventually won the final. Markíza is the third available channel.

As an antidote to the dry, dull programmes of the socialist era, the commercial stations (such as Markíza and JOJ) offer fairly dumbed-down evening entertainment, with a ratings-winning selection of game shows, reality TV and soap operas. **Markíza** (*www.markiza.sk*) is a privately owned commercial station, the most popular station in the region at the moment. One of Markíza's most popular shows was *Mojsejovci*, the reality programme where about 15 youngsters moved into the garage of a former rock star and his much older rich wife and lived in *Big Brother*-style togetherness, with contestants voted off by the public each week. The prize money was seductive at two million koruna.

JOJ (*www.joj.sk*) is a commercial Slovak station, local to Bratislava, with cheap programmes, attempting to challenge Markíza. It shows a lot of sports live and **NOVA** shows news, soap operas and films. **Prima** shows sports and American soap operas while **TA3** (*www.ta3.com*) is a Slovak news channel. The Czech channels **ČT1** and **ČT2** show a lot of bizarre local soap operas where characters spend the entire time checking and reciting text messages. Hungarian stations **RTL Klub** and **MTV1** and **MTV2** are all available.

Being situated right in the heart of central Europe, Slovak TVs can also pick up broadcasts from TV stations in Poland, Germany and Austria.

Radio

Radio Okey (*www.okey.sk*) is part of the TV Markíza group, set up a few years back under the name Radio Koliba. Radio Okey is now the most listened-to station in Bratislava.

Radio Slovensko is broadcast by Slovenský Rozhlas (*www.slovakradio.sk*) from the wonderful inverted pyramid building on Mýtna just north of Námestie Slobody. Slovak Radio operates five national networks (Slovensko, Devín, FM, Regina, Patria) and an external service.

Radio Slovakia International started broadcasting in English in March 1993. In the daily 30-minute spots, they broadcast news and extensive information on all aspects of life in Slovakia. Listeners can tune into Radio Slovakia International worldwide on shortwave via the World Radio Network or the internet (*www.wrn.org*).

Private radio stations competing for listeners in Bratislava include **Radio Expres** (*www.expres.sk*), doing well recently after purchase by an international communications group, **Radio Regina** (*www.radioregina.sk*), **Fun Radio** (*www.funradio.sk*) and **Radio Twist** (*www.twist.sk*).

COMMUNICATIONS
Telephone and fax
Cheap local calls can be made from any phone, but for international calls use a card phone; buy a card (*telefonná karta*) from a tobacconist or post office.

Bratislava's area code is 02 (remove the zero when calling from outside Slovakia). Bratislava telephone numbers are eight digits long (after the 02). For calling cell phones, the numbers usually begin with 0903, 0904, 0905 etc followed by a six-digit number.

Communications

For calls out of the country, dial the international access code '00', listen for the second burring tone, and proceed with the relevant country code and number. Some country codes (including Slovakia's) are listed overleaf:

Australia	61	Germany	49	Poland	48
Austria	43	Greece	30	Slovakia	421
Belgium	32	Hungary	36	Spain	34
Canada	1	Ireland	353	UK	44
France	33	Italy	39	USA	1

Emergency telephone numbers
Police 158
City police 159
Ambulance 155 (emergency contact in English 112)
Fire brigade 150 (emergency contact in English 112)
Autoclub helpline (ASA Slovakia) 0123
Emergency road service 0154
Assistance for motorists 18 124

Other useful numbers
Local directory enquiries 0120
International directory enquiries 12 149
Recently changed numbers 0128

Practicalities

Tourist information 02 5443 3715
Eurolines international bus transport 02 5542 4870
Information on air transport 02 4857 3353

Post offices

Most post offices (*pošta*) open Monday–Friday 08.00–17.00. You can also buy stamps (*známky*) from some tobacconists (*tabák*) and street kiosks. Poste restante is available in major towns; write Pošta 1 (the main office), followed by the name of the town. The main post office at Námestie SNP 34–35 is open Monday–Friday 07.00–20.00, Saturday 07.00–18.00, Sunday 09.00–14.00. See *Language* chapter (page 232) for letter-sending vocabulary.

Internet

Internet cafés have sprouted up all over Bratislava; expect to pay 60–120Sk/hr.

Many hotels either offer WiFi connections in rooms (for a fee) or some have free WiFi zones in their cafés and lobbies. Many hotels also offer fast broadband internet although if you are staying in an expensive hotel, the internet charge will be commensurately dearer and you'd be better off sitting in a café, accompanying your correspondence with a cold beer.

Internet cafés

Impetus Michalská 2. Central internet café offering copy services. Internet 1Sk/min. *Open daily 08.00–23.00.*

Communications

Internet Centrum Michalská 2. Has five machines. *Open daily 09.00–midnight.*

Kristián Pub Michalská 10; ↖ 02 5443 4038. Five fast machines, internet power: 1,500kb, 1Sk/min. *Open daily 14.00–midnight.*

London Café Panská 17. Two free machines in the British Council café.

Mamutnet.sk at Sparx ↖ 02 5263 1011; www.mamutnet.sk. Dozens of machines at Cintorínska 32, entrance at Ferienčíkova ulica; costs 60Sk/hr but about half that amount if you register. Scanning, printing, copying, burning and WiFi. *Open daily 10.00–04.00.*

Megainet Klariská 4. Six machines, coffee, beer, internet 1Sk/min (minimum 10 mins), Vlastne Hotspot WIFI 2Sk/min, 40Sk/15 min, 120Sk/60 min, 200Sk/120 min. Scanning costs 20Sk per A4 sheet, photocopying costs 2Sk per A4 sheet. Cappuccino 40Sk, Zlaty Bažant 39Sk for 330ml.

Net Café Baštová 9. Has just one machine; very loud music.

Slovak Telecom Bar Námestie Slobody. In the Telecom hut.

Speedy Pub Obchodná 48; ↖ 0904 999 999. *Open Mon–Fri 09.30–02.00, Sat 10.00–02.00, Sun 11.30–midnight.*

EMBASSIES AND CONSULATES IN BRATISLAVA

Austria (Rakúske veľvyslanestvo) Ventúrska 10; ↖ 02 5930 1500; f 02 5443 2486; e pressburg-ob@bmaa.gv.at; www.embassyaustria.sk. *Open Mon–Fri 08.00–12.00.*

Canada (in Prague) Muchova 6, 160 00 Praha 6, Czech Republic; ↖ +420 27210 1800; e Canada@canada.cz; www.canada.cz. *Office hours Mon–Fri 08.30–12.30, 13.30–16.30; consular section open Mon–Fri 08.30–12.30.*

Office of the Canadian Embassy in Bratislava Carlton Courtyard and Savoy Building, Mostová 2; ☏ 02 5920 4031; f 02 5443 4227; e brslva@international.gc.ca. *Office open Mon–Fri 08.30–12.00, 13.30–16.30.*

Czech Republic Hviezdoslavovo námestie 8, PO Box 208; ☏ 02 5920 3303; f 02 5920 3330; e bratislava@embassy.mzv.cz; www.mzv.cz/bratislava. *Open Mon–Thu 09.00–11.00 (receiving documents), Mon–Thu 11.00–12.00 (issuing documents).*

European Union Panská 3; ☏ 02 5443 1718; e delegation-slovakia@cec.eu.int; www.europa.sk; representation office at Palisády 29; ☏ 02 5443 1718.

France Hlavné námestie 7; ☏ 02 5934 7111; f 02 5934 7199; e consulat.bratislava-amba@diplomatie.gouv.fr; http://france.sk/ambassade. *Office hours Mon–Fri 09.00–12.00; visa inquiries on Mon, Wed & Fri 09.00–12.00.*

Germany Hviezdoslavovo námestie. 10; ☏ 02 5920 4400; f 02 5441 9634; e public@germanembassy.sk; www.germanembassy.sk. *Telephone enquiries on 02 5920 4444 Mon–Fri 08.30–11.30.*

Hungary Sedlárska 3, 814 25 Bratislava; ☏ 02 5920 5200; f 02 5443 5484; e pozsony@emnhung.sk. *Consular section open Mon, Wed & Thu 08.30–11.30.*

Ireland Carlton Savoy Building, Mostová 2; ☏ 02 5930 9611; f 02 5443 0690; Bratislava@iveagh.irlgov.ie; enquiries on the hotline ☏ 02 5443 0690. *Office hours Mon–Fri 09.00–12.30, 14.30–16.30*

Russia Godrova 4; ☏ 02 5441 4664; e konzulat@chello.sk; www.slovakia.mid.ru. *Consular section open Mon, Wed & Fri 09.00–12.00.*

South Africa Révova 27; ☏ 02 5441 7841; f 02 5441 7853; e mlopasov@jacsk.jnj.com;

Embassies and consulates

www.saembvie.at. Consulate based in Vienna at Sandgasse 33.

UK Panská 16; ℡ 02 5998 2000; f 02 5998 2237; e bebra@internet.sk;
www.britishembasssy.sk. *Office hours Mon–Fri 08.30–17.00, consulate and visa section open Mon–Fri 09.00–12.00, 14.00–15.30.*

Ukraine Radvanská 35; ℡ 02 5920 2816; f 02 5920 2837; e ukremb@ukrembassy.sk;
www.ukrembassy.sk. *Consulate open Mon–Wed & Fri 08.30–11.30 (receiving documents), 14.00–15.00 (issuing documents), closed Thu.*

USA Hviezdoslavovo námestie 4; ℡ + 02 5443 3338; f 02 5443 0096;
e arc_brat@pd.state.gov; www.usembassy.sk. *Consular section open for American citizens Mon–Fri 08.00–12.00, 14.00–15.30, closed at weekends and for American and Slovak public holidays. In the event of a genuine emergency, you can reach the Embassy Duty Officer after working hours, on holidays and weekends m 0903 703 666.*

RELIGIOUS SERVICES

The Bratislava International Church holds English-language worship every Sunday at 09.30 at the Small Lutheran Church (Malý evanjelický kostól) in central Bratislava on Lýcejná ulica at the intersection with Panenská 26/28 (near the Crowne Plaza Hotel). Children's Sunday School also provided. ℡ 02 5443 3263; www.evangelical.sk.

The International Church of Bratislava holds English-language worship every Sunday at 10.00 in the building of 'Únia žien' at Štefánikova 4. Children's programme also available. For more information contact Pete and Vierka Miller on 02 6596 7512.

TOURIST INFORMATION

BKIS Bratislava Cultural and Information Centre Klobučnícka 2; ☎ 02 5441 5801; f 02 5441 5348; e bkis@bkis.sk; www.bkis.sk. *Open Jun–Sep Mon–Fri 08.30–19.00, Sat–Sun 09.00–17.00; Oct–May Mon–Fri 08.30––18.00, Sat 09.00–15.00, Sun 10.00–15.00.*

BKIS Klobučnícka 2; ☎ 02 5443 3715. There is also a shop inside the BKIS office offering a range of maps, postcards, small folk crafts and books on Bratislava. BKIS offers help with: *Accommodation* in Bratislava, ☎ 02 5443 3715; *Guides* to walking, sightseeing (in 13 languages); *Thematic walks* through the historic centre; *Sightseeing* in a historic street car (Jun–Aug); *Sightseeing* in town (reservations required); *Trips* to the surrounding countryside, ☎ 02 5443 4059; f 02 5443 2708; *Translation and interpreting* services, ☎ 02 5443 4059; f 02 5443 2708; *Trips* and walks, ☎ 02 5443 1707; f 02 5443 2708; *Adrenalin programmes*, ☎ 02 5443 1707; f 02 5443 2708; *Ticket office* for cultural events in Slovakia or abroad, ☎ 02 5443 2708; *Organisation* of cultural and social events with technical services and catering, ☎ 02 5441 4048; f 02 5441 5348.

BKIS at main railway station Hlavná stanica; ☎ 02 5249 5906. *Open Jun–Sep Mon–Fri 08.00–19.30, Sat–Sun 08.00–16.30; Oct–May Mon–Fri 08.30–17.00, Sat–Sun 09.00–14.00.*

BKIS at M R Štefánik Airport *Open Jun–Sep Mon–Fri 10.00––19.00, Sat–Sun 10.00–18.00; Oct–May Mon–Fri 09.00–19.00, Sat–Sun 10.00–18.00.*

BKIS at Passenger Port (Tourist Information Centre of BKIS) Fajnorovo nábrežie 2. *Open May–Sep Mon–Sat 10.00–17.00, Sun 10.00–16.00.*

BTS (Bratislava Tourist Service) Ventúrska 9; ☎ 02 5464 1794, m 0900 211 221; www.bratislava-info.sk. This office is not connected to BKIS but provides similar services:

hotel leaflets, guide books, postcards, T-shirts, coins. Information is given in English, German, Slovak, Czech, French, Italian and Russian. They operate guided tours daily at 14.00 (two-hour-long tours) for 450Sk (€12) per person in English. Tours in German Fri–Sun at 14.00 also 450Sk (€12) per person. *Apr–Oct open daily 10.00–20.00, Nov–Mar open daily 10.00–16.00.*

LOCAL TOURS

Organised tours can take you around town on foot, by bicycle or even on a little bus/train contraption.

City tour on little red bus/train in the Old Town; ⌕ 0903 302 817. Leaves from Hlavné námestie. Costs 200Sk (€6) per person; tour takes 30 minutes, in English, German, French, Spanish.

Bratislava guided pub crawl Enquiries at info@bratislavaguide.com. With Bratislava guide explore the local pub and bar scene. Sample the most popular, glamorous or authentic venues. Wine and dine guides also available. Cost from 399Sk (€10.50) per person, group rates available.

Guided bicycle tour ⌕ 0907 683 112; e info@bratislavasightseeing.com; www.bratislavasightseeing.com. Organised by Luka Tours; also trips to Devín Castle, the Small Carpathian Wine Route, cycle tour along the river Morava floodplain.

Boat trips Fajnorovo nábrežie 2; ⌕ 02 5293 2226; e travel@lod.sk; www.lod.sk for trips from Bratislava. From Devín you can take a boat across to Hainburg in Austria (see *Beyond the City*, page 228 for details).

Wine tour The local travel agents (below) can organise trips along the Small Carpathian Wine Route.

LOCAL TRAVEL AGENTS

Local travel agents can help with trips out of town, accommodation, excursions and car rental. They also have endless supplies of pamphlets about Slovakia.

Oneworld Travel Ulica 29 augusta 2; ✆ 02 5273 1202; f 02 5273 1205; e oneworld@oneworldtravel.sk; www.oneworldtravel.sk. Can arrange accommodation in Bratislava and other Slovak cities, tailor-made services for individuals and groups, special-interest tours, conferences and business conventions, sports and cultural events, transfers, wine tastings, accommodation and services in Prague, Vienna and Budapest, reservation and sale of airline tickets.

Slovakia Green Tours Radlinského 27; ✆ 02 5249 1641; f 02 5249 1651; e contact@slovakiagreentours.com; www.slovakiagreentours.com. Slovakia Green Tours is a family-run company established at the beginning of 2003 to promote Slovakia as a viable destination for nature lovers, hikers, photographers, lovers of beautiful scenery and lovers of life. They also do well-organised stag and hen tours.

Bratislava Stags Radlinského 27; ✆ 02 5245 1441; f 02 5249 1651; e info@bratislavastags.com; www.bratislavastags.com. Dean Cobbold is involved with Green Tours, Bratislava Stags and most of the partying that goes on in town. He has a new service at: www.stayslovakia.com helping visitors find hotels and eventually dealing with all of Slovakia. *Open Mon–Fri 09.00–18.00, Sat 09.00–13.00.*

Stag Bratislava Pribinova 23; ☏ 0903 717 899; f 02 5921 0106; e info@stagbratislava.com; www.stagbratislava.com. Run by three Slovak ladies: Barbara and the team, a family business since 2000.

Omega Tours Panská 12; ☏ 02 5443 1367; f 02 5443 1541; e omegatours@omegatours.sk; www.omegatours.sk. In business since 1995. Offers tailor-made tours, four-capital tours (Prague, Budapest, Vienna, Bratislava), Danube cruises, Discover Slovakia tours, day trips such as Bratislava Halfday Sightseeing Tour, Danube Cruise & Devín Castle, the Small Carpathian Wine Route and a typical Slovak dinner with live music. They also offer airport transfer Bratislava–Vienna (1,500Sk/€37).

ITC Travel Štefánikova 29; ☏ 02 5249 4593; www.itctravel.sk and www.itc-traveller.com. Offer complete opera and weekend packages to Bratislava.

Limba Michalská 3; ☏ 02 5441 8601; f 02 5920 6969; e limba@limba.sk; www.limba.sk. Has a great selection of mountain huts (*chata*) and cottages. Also family boarding houses, bungalows, hotels and spas.

SATUR (Slovak National Tourist Board) Miletičova 1; ☏ 02 5542 2828; f 02 5556 1426; e info@acr.satur.sk; www.satur.sk. Organises guided tours around Bratislava and day trips to the Small Carpathian Wine Route, Červený Kameň, or dinner in a traditional restaurant.

DISCOUNT CARD

For getting the best out of the city, the **Bratislava City Card** (*www.bratislavacitycard.sk*) is a great idea. Produced by BKIS, the city tourist office (*www.bkis.sk*) and City Hall (*www.bratislava.sk*), it offers a free guided city tour,

WEIGHT AND GRAVITY

There is an obsession in Bratislava with weight and gravity. Meat dishes (but also vegetables, fish, pasta, rice) are all listed in restaurants with their weight given in grams. Whole fish, like trout and carp, are listed with prices for an average fish, then 7–10Sk added on for each extra decagram weight of raw fish. So, unless you specify that you only want a little fish, you may end up paying a couple of euros more than you expected.

Beer is always listed with its specific gravity measured at degrees Plato (the German engineer, not the Greek philosopher) usually 10° or 12°. This is NOT the same as the percentage of alcohol, otherwise we'd be totally smashed drinking half-litres of Zlaty Bazant (if 12° was confused with 12%, the same strength as red wine) at lunchtime.

discounts on taxis, entry to Bratislava Zoo, the Municipal Museum, swimming pools and some restaurants as well as other guided tours and trips. Cards are valid for one (€5), two (€8) or three (€10) days and are available from all the BKIS offices: at the airport, ferry port, railway station and in Klobučnícka (Central Tourist Point) in the Old Town centre. They can also be found in some participating hotels. The card is validated when a member of BKIS staff signs and dates it at one of their offices.

PUBLIC TOILETS

Apart from nipping into a pub, you'll find there is a dearth of places to spend a koruna, and you'll need one after all that lager. The subway under Hodžovo námestie, the bus and railway stations all have public toilets, some more gruesome than others. The public convenience at the back of the bus station under Nový most (New Bridge) is not nearly as dreadful as it first appears. It's quite clean and with an attendant keeping an eye on matters. Pubs and restaurants such as Dubliners and Kristián pub are not too grumpy about people using the loo without buying a drink. McDonald's at Gorkého 1, at the corner of Hviezdoslavovo námestie, is a good place to use the bathroom (downstairs and to the left).

Local transport

PUBLIC TRANSPORT

A metro system has been in the planning for many years to ease congestion in the centre when all the cars come in. Tickets for the present system of trams, buses and trolleybuses are based on an honour system. Plain-clothed inspectors prowl the trams, although they are hardly ever spotted. As the transport system is so well organised with buses, trams and trolleys all linking up, they all run on time, are comfortable and clean and the prices are staggeringly low. Therefore visitors should buy (and stamp) a ticket to give encouragement.

There's a route planner at www.imhd.sk with a brief history of Bratislava transport and the Bratislava transport company is at www.dpb.sk.

The **ticket machines** offer 15 possibilities – some in English and German as well as Slovak; these are the usual ones:

Basic ticket 10 minutes	14Sk
Basic ticket 30 minutes (45 mins at weekends/holidays!)	18Sk
Basic ticket 60 minutes	22Sk
Tourist 24 hours both zones	90Sk
Tourist 48 hours both zones	170Sk
Tourist 3 days both zones	210Sk

There are two zones in Bratislava based on concentric circles. I would suggest always buying the 30-minute ticket costing less than 50p (45 minutes at weekends/holidays) because you can get anywhere in the city within 30 minutes (with the exception of Zlaté Piesky which is in zone (*pasmo*) 2 and requires a second ticket. You may be able to get away with using the 30-minute ticket, but for peace of mind you can pay 4Sk more for an hour's ticket.

Trams

There are 13 tram routes running all around town, numbered 1–17 (with a few missing numbers). Be aware that some trams (like number 14) run on one continuous loop (not on two lanes going forward and back), so the route going home to the hotel may not follow the same streets as you came in on, especially in town.

Buses

There are 63 bus routes, numbered 20–198 (with a few missing numbers), and 18 nightbus routes, numbered 501–518. These all link up well with the trams and trolleys, and services run on time. Probably the bus route you will use the most is the 29 to Devín.

Trolleybuses

There are 11 trolleybus routes, numbered 201–212, running mostly in the hills and northern parts of town. Trolleys also can go around in a loop and come back on a different route from the way you went.

Airport transfer

See *Getting there and away* section.

Taxis

Some say local taxi drivers are a brat pack who rip off foreigners at every possible occasion. This stereotype is a little out-dated, and all those I met were courteous, extremely friendly and helpful. One was most hurt when I asked about the fare before getting in, and pointed to the meter as if his honour was being challenged. Taxis around the city should cost 200–400Sk, whilst from the city to the airport is 300–400Sk. From the city to Vienna Airport costs 2,500–2,800Sk. Some reputable firms are listed below:

ABC taxis ⤸ 02 161 00
Airport Taxi Service ⤸ 02 4364 3033
Euro Taxi ⤸ 02 160 22
Milan Gálik, Profi Taxi ⤸ 02 162 22; 24hr service on 0903 768 666; 0905 768 666 (cost 200Sk within town)
VIP taxis ⤸ 02 160 00

CAR RENTAL

The rates of Slovak car-rental agencies are substantially cheaper than those of Western firms, ranging from 690Sk to 1,500Sk per day and the process is marked by much less red tape.

Ab-Wickam Kopcianska 65; ☎ 0905 653 551 (office hours), hotline: 0903 655 390; e info@ab-wickam.sk; www.ab-wickam.sk. Operating long-term and short-term rent-a-car since 2001, with Škoda Fabias from 590Sk/day, Volkswagen Golfs from 1,240Sk/day.

Auto Rotos Račianska 184/B; ☎ 02 4487 2666; e pozicovna@auto-rotos.sk; www.autorotos.sk. Good deals available with Škodas; the Fabia from 600Sk, the Octavia from 1,500Sk/day. *Open Mon–Fri 08.00–18.00, Sat 08.30–14.00.*

Avis ☎ 02 5341 6111; www.avis.sk. Cars available from Bratislava M R Štefánik Airport, Hotel Danube, Crowne Plaza, Radisson SAS Carlton Hotel. Opel Corsas available from €51/day, Mercedes Benz A140 from €70/day.

Europcar M R Štefánik Airport; ☎ 02 4926 2637; e europcar@porsche.sk; www.europcar.sk. Volkswagen Golf costs €874/week. *Office open Mon–Fri 08.00–18.00, Sat–Sun 24hr opening.*

Hertz M R Štefánik Airport; ☎ 02 4329 1482; e hertz@hertz.sk; www.hertz.sk. Opel Corsas from 1,210Sk/day, Škoda Octavias from 2,680Sk/day.

Sixt M R Štefánik Airport; ☎ 02 4824 5178; 24hr service on 0903 732 292; www.e-sixt.co.uk. Ford Fiestas from 9,210Sk/week.

Parking in Bratislava

As the centre is car-free and the surrounding streets clogged with cars, it's useful to know where to leave the motor safely – a lot of towing and wheel clamping goes on.

Radisson SAS Carlton Hotel underground parking Hviezdoslavovo námestie. Open 07.00–01.00, 420 places, 30Sk/hr.

Hotel Danube parking garage Rybné námestie. Open non-stop, 130 places, fee: 07.00–19.00 55Sk/hr, 19.00–07.00 35Sk/hr.

Hotel Danube car park Open non-stop, 41 places, fee: 07.00–19.00 50Sk/hr, 19.00–07.00 30Sk/hr.

DANUBE RIVER CRUISES

Taking a river cruise to Budapest or Vienna is a lovely way to spend an afternoon.

Visitors arrive in Bratislava by **hydrofoil** (*www.lod.sk*), down the Danube from Vienna or upstream from Budapest. If you're going from Budapest, check out www.mahartpassnave.hu.

International connections on larger cruise boats from Austria and Hungary are possible on the Danube, which is also linked with the Rhine, the Black Sea and the Main. For sales and ticket information, ✆ 02 5293 2226.

For charter of cruise vessels and catering services, ✆ 02 5293 2224. For online booking check out www.lod.sk.

The **docking area** is near to the centre, five minutes' walk from Hviezdoslavovo námestie at Fajnorovo nábrežie 2 [4 E7]. Walk past the Reduta towards the Danube then turn left and walk along the embankment.

International cruises to Vienna cost 720Sk return, 550Sk one way. International cruises to Budapest cost €89 return, €69 one way.

Trips to Gabčíkovo hydro-electric plant from 30 April to 24 September cost 450Sk adult, 300Sk child. Bratislava round-trip sightseeing boat from 27 April to 18 September costs 95Sk adult, 60Sk child. Trips to Devín are daily except Mondays from 26 April to 18 September cost 140/95Sk adult, 95/80Sk child.

The shipping company **Lod** can also organise sightseeing boats, yachting excursions and a restaurant boat.

Accommodation

INTRODUCTION

Since the Velvet Divorce from the Czech Republic in 1993, Slovakia has been working really hard to get its house in order. Bratislava's Old Town has had a wash and brush up and most of the hotels have also buffed up their buildings, improved amenities and gone all out to attract the anticipated flood of visitors.

For a relatively small city, Bratislava has more than its fair share of hotels competing for tourists, business visitors and local travellers, making for a healthy atmosphere of each hotel, pension or hostel trying to outdo the others in terms of facilities, prices and bathroom freebies. Interestingly, there are actually many more higher-range hotels than budget accommodation. While this doesn't mean it will be overpriced, by Western standards, it ensures reasonable quality throughout, which is reassuring. Most hotels are three star and four star in Bratislava.

There is still a wide variety of accommodation, however, giving the visitor a good choice when considering location, amenities, theme even, as with the gimmicky-yet-fun Film Hotel. While we're on the topic of theme, some people go to the former Eastern Bloc countries in search of the bad old days of the former regime. If Soviet nostalgia is your bag, you're in luck.

Few reminders of the old surly socialist days remain in hotel architecture and style of service. As far as décor goes, some hotels such as the high-rise Hotel Kyjev and Hotel Sorea, a former trade union watering hole, can really only be recommended for venue, low price and to those who want to wallow in retro communist chic.

Like many in the region, the Slovak hoteliers are fixated about the star system of grading hotels, another hangover from the communist mania for points-scoring, be it ice skating or extra marks for those creepy welcome messages that spring into life on the TV screen when you enter your new bedroom.

I never met anybody who could accurately explain to me the starring system, but if you are one of those in the know, it apparently gives an indication as to services, amenities and standard of interior, but sometimes it seems quite arbitrary.

There is a bunch of really excellent four-star hotels in Bratislava, yet none makes it to that yearned-for five-star level. Apparently the Radisson SAS Carlton Hotel was only denied its five stars because it is in a historic, protected building and so the new owners could not reconstruct it to provide a separate bathroom and toilet for every room.

I have therefore singled out a trio of four-star hotels which stand out from the crowd and give that little extra pampering. If my budget allowed, I'd plump for a pillow in one of these three any day, or night. In the next two years, two more luxury hotels will be constructed and hope to join this elite trio; both are situated beside the Danube, one in the River Park district and one in Pribinova.

As far as the other four-star hotels are concerned, there is something to suit all tastes, with a range of facilities, styles and locations. Some of the best-established, more traditional top-class hotels are situated on the Danube banks, with a view of the river and the UFO café hovering above a bridge. Some are even right on the river. There are three 'botels' – hotels on boats – in Bratislava, with varying styles and sizes of cabin, facilities and attitude. Some smaller, yet no less chi-chi guesthouses can be found in the hilly residential area to the north of the city's Old Town heart and some are quite a hike away, in the more modern districts, usually heading towards Bratislava's M R Štefánik Airport, 9km northeast of town.

There are also a number of mid-range hotels, usually lurking around the three-star level and many found outside the Old Town in less attractive parts of the city. These can be fun if you don't mind negotiating a tram ride each morning and evening and also give a glimpse of Slovak life beyond the tourist belt. The hotels situated towards the airport in sprawling housing districts such as Ružinov tend to cater for business travellers, and have a good range of services such as high-speed internet connections and fitness centres. These offer bargain rates at weekends for the leisure traveller and are popular with young families on a tighter budget.

The hotels have been sorted into price range, beginning with the luxury trio and following on with the four star, three star, two star and one star. The listing of hotels within each category is purely alphabetical. Some older hotels list their rates only in koruna. Where this occurs, a euro equivalent is also given. (Newer, business hotels often deal only in euros.)

Bratislava is not such a huge city so hotels, pensions, hostels, private apartments and campsites are not divided into district, and only the hotel section is separated into five price categories. Bus (B̲), tram (T̲), trolleybus (T̲B̲) and nightbus (N̲B̲) numbers are also shown.

introduction

The prices given are walk-in rates for a double room during high season – generally May–October and the period over New Year. During low season rates drop by around 30%. As for paying, all the hotels listed of three-star status and above accept the major credit cards; check with others first about methods of payment. The 19% VAT (DPH) is often added to the charge, but where it is extra, it is noted. Likewise, there is a city tourist tax (€0.50–1.00 per person per night) which some hotels add on after and some include. Advance reservations, group bookings, and stays of more than one night will bring room charges down, and with the hot competition for guests, almost all hotels above three stars offer discounted deals on weekend breaks. If travelling independently, keep an eye on websites like www.lastminute.com and www.expedia.com.

The facilities you can expect in each category are laid out below. Breakfast is a buffet spread of cereal, fruit, bread, salami and cheese, tomatoes and peppers, scrambled egg, frankfurters and hot spicy sausage, with a selection of tea, coffee and juice.

Many hotels can arrange bike hire, opera trips and other excursions.

HOTELS
Luxury

These three are officially rated as four-star hotels, but the Crowne Plaza, Marrol's and Radisson SAS Carlton soar so high above all others that they deserve a separate category. These three all have great, if varying, locations near the centre, en-suite rooms with a bath and/or shower, television with satellite channels and pay-per-view movies (in Slovak, German and English), telephone, minibar, room safe, air conditioning, internet-access point or business centre, restaurant and bar, fitness facilities and sauna; they may also have a swimming pool, solarium, shops and café.

Crowne Plaza Hotel Bratislava Hodžovo námestie 2; ☏ 02 5934 8111; f 02 5443 3265; e cp.bratislava@ichotelsgroup.com; www.ichotelsgroup.com/h/d/6c/1/en/hd/btsha [1 C1, 2 D3] B̄ *31, 34, 39, 59, 94;* T̄B̄ *203, 205, 206, 208*

Good location just north of the Old Town, opposite the Presidential Palace of Grasalkovič, where the busy Staromestská highway zooms across Hodžovo námestie. French architects built this former Forum Hotel in the 1980s, and unfortunately from the outside, it shows. It can't shake off its hideous shell but makes valiant efforts indoors. It was completely renovated and regenerated in 2004 and opened as the Crowne Plaza in June 2005. With its state-of-the-art technical equipment and excellent business services, a pool, fitness centre and a two-in-one restaurant (the Magd a Lena), the hotel attracts both business folk and those seeking a little extra pampering while on holiday. 223 guest rooms and suites, 14 meeting rooms, health centre with sauna and whirlpool. Sgl from 5,631Sk (€145), dbl 6,020–7,767Sk (€155–200).

Hotel Marrol's Tobrucká 4; ☏ 02 5778 4600; f 02 5778 4601; e rec@hotelmarrols.sk; www.hotelmarrols.sk [1 D4, 5 F6] B̄ *50;* T̄ *1, 4, 11, 12, 14*

Hotel Marrol's is a gem of a hotel, hiding away in a modest terraced building on a back street, five minutes' walk from Hviezdoslavovo námestie. It feels more like staying in

Hotels

somebody's luxury home, as this boutique hotel spares no expense to create a feeling of comfort and effortless style. The lobby is more like a private living room, with walls lined with bookshelves and plush carpets. The rooms divide into two categories – quality and executive – and there are also 'ladies' chambers' with a more feminine touch. The apartments are pretty swanky also, with suites in varying levels of luxury. The Medina restaurant already has a great reputation around town for its Italian dishes and quality wine list and the Jasmine spa offers a retreat from the hectic business of the day. The staff make great efforts to please and the beds are very comfortable. 16 sgls, 23 dbls, 3 twins. Buffet breakfast not included in price (300Sk a day) and local city tax also extra (30Sk per person per day). Weekend packages available from 14,000Sk for two people two nights, 12,500Sk 'senior citizen' weekend specials. Quality sgl 6,100Sk (€157), quality dbl 6,700Sk (€172), executive dbl 8,700Sk (€224), ladies' chamber 6,100Sk (€157), apts 10,200–19,900Sk (€262–512).

Radisson SAS Carlton Hotel Hviezdoslavovo námestie 3; ✆ 02 5939 0000; f 02 5939 0010; e reservation.bratislava@radissonsas.com; www.radissonsas.com [1 C4, 4 E6] T̅ 1, 4, 11, 12, 14
For location alone, this vast imposing hotel overlooking Hviezdoslavovo námestie wins hands down. The present building dates from 1912, when hotelier Henry Pruger created a Carlton–Savoy complex on the site of the Three Green Trees inn. It closed for reconstruction in 1992 and re-opened nine years later as part of the Radisson SAS group. Less than a minute's walk from the Opera House and Reduta and two from the Old Town,

the Carlton has plush, chintzy furnishings and original glass atrium ceilings. Bedrooms come in two styles, the warmer, traditional golden hues or the modern, cooler colours. The bar has a homely, albeit smoky, ambience and the Opera Brasserie restaurant has changing foodie concepts. Fabulous buffet breakfast. Well-appointed fitness centre (all free for guests, except massage) where apparently David Beckham enjoyed the sports massage (60mins/1,100Sk €28) so much he went back for seconds. Finnish sauna and steam room. WiFi internet (290Sk/hour) available in every room. Kettles and complimentary herbal teas plus a vast selection of bathroom smellies in all rooms make guests feel really special. Parking in underground garage. 168 dbls/sgls, 5 suites, 3 junior suites, 1 unique room at number 127, the Maria Theresia Room, reconstructed from that era for honeymooners but with separate beds, as was the custom then. Weekend specials €160. Sgl 7,100Sk (€182), dbl 7,500Sk (€193), suites 11,900Sk (€306).

Four-star

There are some top-class centrally located hotels available, some of them situated directly in the Old Town. Some are located on a hill north of town in a calm green residential area, yet still very close to the Old Town and accessible by both car and public transport. Four-star hotels have the same features as those in the luxury section, but may not have such good locations or restaurants. They will have en-suite rooms with a bath and/or shower, television with satellite channels, telephone, minibar, room safe, air conditioning, business centre with internet access, restaurant and bar, and many also have fitness facilities.

Hotels

Best Western Hotel West Koliba-Kamzík les; ✆ 02 5478 8692; f 02 5477 7781;
e hotel@hotel-west.sk; www.hotel-west.sk
TB *203 from Hodžovo námestie, in front of Crowne Plaza to terminus;* NB *516; by car or taxi in 15 minutes from the town centre.*
Beautiful location on top of wooded hills north of the city, but not very convenient for guests without cars, as the walk from the bus/trolley stop is about a mile down, or up, a steep yet scenic mountain trail. Close enough to town for business folk but yet peaceful and separate from the city. A young, modern hotel surrounded by great hiking hills. Individually furnished apartments for those staying a little longer with kitchen and direct phone lines. Restaurant offers Slovak and Mexican dishes. During the summer barbecues are held on the terrace. Conference rooms with capacity of 15 or 40 seats. Sauna, small pool, sunbathing studio. Hiking, mountain-biking, tennis courts nearby. Nightclub for meetings or parties. 100 beds. Dbl economy 3,300Sk (€85), dbl standard 3,500Sk (€90), dbl superior 4,000Sk (€103), suite 5,000Sk (€129), penthouse 6,000Sk (€155). City tax of 15Sk (€0.40) is extra. Breakfast included.

Botel Marína Nábrežie arm. gen. Ľ. Svobodu; ✆ 02 5464 1804; f 02 5464 1771;
e info@botelmarina.sk; www.botelmarina.sk [4 A7]
T *1, 4, 12;* B *29, 30, 70, 80, 90;* NB *502*
Conveniently situated for the Old Town, a ten-minute walk heading upstream along the Danube embankment. A botel is a hotel on a boat, except that sometimes they aren't real boats, just engine-less barges. This one was a real boat, however, originally berthed in

Budapest then tugged upstream to
accommodate visitors to Bratislava.
Botel Marína opened in July 2004 with
small, claustrophobic twin cabins, Staying
on a boat is a great experience, especially
sleeping on the famous Danube, with the water
gently rocking guests to sleep; however it's obvious this
was not a purpose-built hotel as it is extremely noisy,
especially at night. The waiters clump across the floorboards of the restaurant on the floor
above and the mooring chains clank at night even when the water is calm. The curtains are
flimsy and offer little privacy. The cleaners begin their vacuuming at 08.30 as if hinting that
getting everything shipshape and Bristol fashion is an all-day job. The miniscule 'wet-style'
bathrooms might not be to everyone's taste; you can wash your feet in the shower while
still sitting on the loo! The restaurant with green-striped wallpaper recalling Habsburg
parlours is better in the evenings, breakfasts are cold and service desultory. There is one
computer at reception with free internet connection, and a helpful receptionist who advises
on sightseeing and travel details. 27 twin rooms with separate beds 2,850Sk (€73), 3 sgls
2,200Sk (€57), 2 suites with dbl beds 3,300Sk (€85). Breakfast included. City tax extra 30Sk
(€0.80).

Holiday Inn Bajkalska 25/A; ↘ 02 4824 5111; f 02 4824 5112; e holidayinn@holidayinn.sk;
www.holiday-inn.com/bratislavasr or try www.holidayinn.sk

Hotels

T 14 *from Námestie Ľ. Štúra to Mraziarenska stop then 8 minutes' walk;* B *68,74,76,198;* NB *509*

The Holiday Inn is handy for the airport, but otherwise it's a bit of a hike getting into town. Situated in an unattractive district, surrounded by petrol stations and housing estates, once you get inside your room, you're not inclined to gaze out of the window. Rooms are furnished and equipped to the traditional Holiday Inn standard: comfortable and spacious. Large choice of eating and drinking venues, a stylish 'Wintergarden' restaurant and a bright brasserie offering excellent buffet breakfasts. Fitness centre with sauna, pool and solarium in the basement (free for guests apart from sauna and solarium; 200Sk). Tennis courts outside. The staff make efforts to be of service. 164 rooms. Sgl & dbl 5,000Sk (€129), apt 8,400Sk (€216). Breakfast included.

Hotel Antares Sulekova 15; ℘ 0910 785 020; f 02 5464 8971; e reservation@hotelantares.sk; www.hotelantares.sk [2 A3]

TB *208 from Hodžovo námestie (in front of Presidential Palace) to the terminus. From Bus station ride trolleybus number 208 to the terminus.* TB *203, 205, 208;* NB *516*

About 15 minutes' walk to the castle, Italian-owned Antares is located in the hilly, residential part, northwest of the Old Town. The hotel is one of the newest in town. (See also nearby Apartment Hotel Sulekova in *Pensions* section.) Part of the Carraro Hotel group offering large bedrooms with modern furniture and fittings, in a stylish Adriatic ambience. All rooms have WiFi internet access. Mini fitness centre with gym, pool, sauna and jacuzzi. Green, quiet surroundings. Sgl €80 (weekend), €100 (weeknight), dbl €90 (weekend), €120

Accommodation

(weeknight), suite €110 (weekend), €150 (weeknight). Breakfast included. City tax 30Sk extra.

Hotel Danube Rybné námestie 1; ✆ 02 5934 0000; f 02 5441 4311; e danube@hoteldanube.com; www.hoteldanube.com [1 B4, 4 D7]
B̲ 29, 30, 37, 70, 71, 80, 90, 91, 191; T̲ 1, 4, 12; N̲B̲ 502

One of the elite group hotels in Bratislava, yet sadly, another of those hideous creations from the socialist era when architects threw all thoughts of aesthetically pleasing buildings out the window in favour of creating in-your-face functionality. From a distance, it looks like it was built with Lego by an unimaginative child. Inside, the rather fussy bedrooms have lavender-and-pink colour schemes and the Romeo e Giulieta restaurant is equally garish with pinky-orange décor, enough to put you off your fettucine. The view from inside is much better with outlooks on to either the river or the castle. Rooms all have cable TV, broadband and WiFi internet access. Non-smoking, family and rooms for disabled visitors also available. Fitness centre with pool, solarium, sauna, massage tables, jacuzzi and aerobics classes. They are justifiably proud of their pastries at the Café Viennois. 276 rooms. Business sgl €185, business dbl €205, executive sgl €215, executive dbl €235, suite (two rooms) €250, apt €300. Breakfast and 19% VAT (DPH) included.

Hotel Devín Riečna 4; ✆ 02 5998 5111; f 02 5443 0682; e recepcia@hoteldevin.sk; www.hoteldevin.sk [1 B/C4, 4 D7]
B̲ 29, 30, 37, 70, 71, 80, 90, 91, 191; T̲ 1, 4, 12; N̲B̲ 502

For many years, Hotel Devín stood alone as the only four-star hotel in Bratislava. It still retains a traditional self-assured ambience and a classic, opulent style. The carpets in the back stairs are a little threadbare but the crystal chandeliers still shimmer. It's one of the best in town and good enough for the Dalai Lama and Vaclav Havel who have both stayed here; not together. The buffet breakfast is superb with great local sausages and cheeses. The flirty waiters don't grasp the concept of cold milk for English tea and give it hot and frothy, often with lemon too, but the service is courteous and charming. Good-sized rooms with very beige marble bathrooms, a woody bar, top-notch restaurant (Francúzska reštaurácia) voted best in town by a Michelin-esque local guide. Centrum Relax fitness centre offers Thai massage, pool, gym, jacuzzi, massage tables, squash courts. Congress hall, meeting rooms, business centre with broadband internet access. Try to get a room at the front, overlooking the river Danube, although those at the back aren't bad either. You can see the castle illuminated in purple at night and St Martin's Cathedral with its bells bonging gently on a Sunday morning. 100 rooms. Sgl € 110–160, dbl € 120–180, junior suite € 250, family suite with kitchen € 300, premier suite (two rooms) € 400. Weekend specials for € 150. Breakfast included.

Hotel Dukla Dulovo námestie 1; ☎ 02 5596 8922; f 02 5596 9815; e dukla@hoteldukla.sk; www.hoteldukla.sk

$\overline{B}$ *50, 82, 85;* $\overline{NB}$ *509*

Situated out to the east of the centre, just beyond the bus station on the main Košická road leading to the brand new Apollo bridge across the Danube. The Dukla was built in the 1960s and was recently refurbished. It has some family connection to Hotel Marrol's but offers a less pricey, less swanky range of accommodation. The rooms are pleasant with TVs and comfortable furnishings. Internet connection (at a fee) in business rooms. The St Hubert (patron saint of hunting) restaurant offers all manner of gamey dishes washed down with Slovak and Moravian wines in a wood-panelled chamber decorated with antlers and bear skins. The kettle in each room is a thoughtful touch. Breakfast 250Sk (€6.55) not incl. Free transfer into town and 20% off restaurant bill for guests at weekends. 104 rooms. Ask a friendly economist to explain the mega-complicated room pricing system. Quality sgl €70–87, business sgl €77–96, small suite for one €108–135, large suite for one €116–145, diplomat suite for one €262–327, quality dbl €76–95, business dbl €87–109, small suite for two €102–128, large suite for two €111–138, diplomat suite €257–321.

Hotel Hradná Brána Slovanské nábrežie 15, Devín; ✆ 02 6010 2511; f 02 6010 2512; e recepcia@hotelhb.sk; www.hotelhb.sk
B̄ 29 from Nový most to terminus
The location, right on the car and coach park, is unfortunate but the general area is delightful, at the confluence of the Danube and Morava rivers and under the towering Devín Castle ruins. It's a good base if you don't mind taking the number 29 bus into town, and also ideal for those who like to do a lot of hiking in fresh air. The hotel is quite new and the interior was given a feng shui session, which may explain the pinky-custardy colours and gentle sloping ceilings. There's a jacuzzi in every bathroom which is a definite plus. All rooms are air conditioned and have under-floor heating. Disabled access. The congress hall 'Štúr' holds 150 business people, and the restaurant Perún offers international cuisine. In

summer guests can enjoy grilled specialities on the terrace with a gorgeous view of Devín Castle. A 'relax centre' has a whirlpool, sauna, solarium, massages and recliner chairs. Naughty Hradná Brána appoints itself five stars; if they are going to have this bizarre system, they should stick to the rules. 12 rooms. Sgl standard €135, dbl standard €155, apt €190 for one, €210 for two, suite €240.

Hotel Kamila Čierna voda 611, Chorvátsky Grob; ☎ 02 4594 3611; f 02 4594 3631; e hotel@kamila.sk; www.kamila.sk

B̄ 53 from Trnavské mýto to Čierna Voda

Situated 10km northeast of the centre, accessible by motorway D1 towards Senec, Hotel Kamila has great views of the Small Carpathian Mountains, but yet guests can get into town in 15 minutes by car (40 minutes by bus). The hotel is owned by well-known Slovak actress Kamila Magálová who stays closely involved in day-to-day operations and makes sure every guest's whim is catered to. Lots of activities and services: golf, tennis, horseriding, wine tasting, folk music, gourmet cuisine. Tasteful, spacious rooms. Wellness centre with Finnish sauna, vertical turbo solarium, cardio-fitness, and an outdoor swimming pool. Massage and aromatherapy. Situated next to an indoor horseback riding hall and a golf course, and offering instruction in both sports. There are jogging opportunities, tennis courts and a billiard room. 5 sgls 3,390Sk (€87), 15 dbls 3,790Sk (€97), 4 suites 4,800Sk (€123). Buffet or à la carte breakfast included. Prices do not include 19% VAT.

Hotel No 16 Partizánska 16a; ☎ 02 5441 1672; f 02 5441 1298; e hotelno16@internet.sk; www.hotelno16.sk [2 A4]

TB *203 or 207 from Hodžovo námestie (in front of Presidential Palace) to Partizánska;* **NB** *516*
Shares a building, up a hill in the leafy, upmarket residential part (Palisády) of town with the consulate of the Republic of Sierra Leone. The garden is filled with expensive sports cars, trees and a high fence guards the ambience of prosperity. The wood-panelled villa is 15 minutes' brisk walk from the Old Town and more personal and charming than larger places. Owned by former Brano Hronec, former pop singer, and Judy Vargova, the hotel's décor recalls a Hansel and Gretel hideaway with wooden beams in every bedroom and a large ceramic stove in the lobby. Imagine the Swiss cottage of a shipping magnate, crammed with a little too much furniture, china and artwork. 16 rooms. Sgl € 100–106, dbl € 110–130, suites € 275. Breakfast included.

Hotel Perugia Zelená 5; ⟍ 02 5443 1818; f 02 5443 1821; e info@perugia.sk; www.perugia.sk [1 B3, 4 D5]
Luxury hotel right in the heart of the Old Town, reconstructed in 1993 by top Slovak architects Dušan Krep and Pavol Suchánek. Designed to suit business travellers, it's also ideal for tourists, given the superb location, amenities and great restaurant. Rooms are plush and pricey with period furniture and original artwork that can be purchased if it appeals. Masseurs arrive from a nearby fitness centre to soothe away stress. Restaurant Gazdovsky Dvor offers Slovak and Hungarian dishes in a rustic stable setting. Situated in the pedestrian zone so no traffic noise, but parking can be problematic and watch out for stag partiers staggering past. 14 rooms. Sgl 4,280Sk (€ 110), dbl 5,080Sk (€ 131), apt 5,660–5,860Sk (€ 146–151). Breakfast included.

Hotels

Three-star

Three-star hotels range from cheaper ones offering good value for money and more expensive ones trying to attract average four-star hotel guests. All have en-suite rooms with bath and/or shower, air conditioning, television and internet access in a business centre. Many also have gyms, fitness centres, eating and drinking venues.

Botel Fairway Nábrežie arm. gen. Ľ. Svobodu; ℡ 02 5442 2090; f 02 5441 2711; e botel@fairway.sk; www.fairway.sk [4 A7]

$\overline{\text{B}}$ 29, 30, 31, 39; $\overline{\text{T}}$ 1, 4, 12; $\overline{\text{NB}}$ 502, 503, 504

Botel Fairway is a squared-off boat, moored further upstream from Botel Marína. The metal three-deck construction is painted white with Miro-esque squiggly designs on its sides. The atmosphere is younger and more relaxed than that in the other two botels. However, it could do with a cleaning lady as enthusiastic as those in the Botel Marína, although maybe not their early-bird tendencies. Sun terrace out on deck in summer. Restaurant with a good selection of international dishes, main courses average out at 140Sk. As it's a little walk to the centre, it doesn't get so many visitors in the evening. Good if you want peace and quiet, but not if you came to party. The gentle rocking aids sleep but it's a bit queasy if your head is already spinning from too much Zlaty Bažant beer. 29 rooms. Sgl 1,800Sk (€46), dbl 2,400Sk (€62). Breakfast included.

Botel Grácia Rázusovo nábrežie; ℡ 02 5443 2132; f 02 5443 2131; e hotel@botel-gracia.sk; www.botel-gracia.sk [4 E7]

Moored nearer to the centre than the other two botels, Botel Grácia is on the Danube near Námestie Ľ. Štúra and just upstream from the ferry dock. It was built as a boat and tugged to this location 14 years ago. Big cabins, much more space than those in the other boats. Enthusiastic staff do their best to make guests feel welcome. In summer the restaurant out on deck is very atmospheric, although you might want to smear on some mosquito cream. The huge suite sleeps six, although you can squeeze in as many as you like, if the kids don't mind sleeping on the floor. Bear in mind that the Cirkus Barok disco boat is moored next door and grooves away until 06.00, so this particular boat might be more suited to those who don't mind noise. 30 rooms. Sgl 2,045Sk (€53), dbl 2,790Sk (€72), suite 8,000Sk (€206). Breakfast included. Can also negotiate on the suite for a lower price for a longer stay.

City Hotel Bratislava Seberíniho 9; ☏ 02 4341 1592; f 02 4333 6420;
e hotel@hotelbratislava.sk; www.hotelbratislava.sk
T̅ 8 (from railway station) 9 (from Kamenné Námestie) 14 (from Námestie Ľštúra) to Tomášikova stop, then five-minute walk; B̅ 50, 86, 96; T̅ 201, 202
Situated in the Ružinov housing district of grey, high-rise 'panelaky' buildings, out towards the airport, City Hotel is three star but with four-star aspirations. Some of the recently renovated business rooms are four star, although they don't match all the separate-bath-and-loo criteria. Built in 1974 as the first 'panelaky' hotel in town, it was known pre-1989 as Hotel Bratislava. In recent years it has put on a new friendly face including professional marketing and customer service. The ten-storey hotel is split right up and down the middle regarding cigarettes; turn left when coming out of the lift and you're in the non-smoking

half, turn right and you're in a cloud of smoke. The rooms are very pleasant with good bathrooms. However, the door springs are too enthusiastic and a lot of slamming goes on at night and early morning. The receptionist tries desperately to maintain a retro effect of the sulky '70s but the waiting staff are courteous and efficient. The WiFi internet access in the bar is free, a bonus as most other hotels charge even for wireless access. It's handy for the airport and extremely popular with business travellers and coach tours, a bit more tricky for individuals until you work out the tram system. Business centre and fitness centre with massage therapy, sauna, whirlpool. Paradise night club. 254 rooms. Standard sgl 2,300Sk (€60), dbl 2,700Sk (€69), business sgl 3,300SK (€85) dbl 3,700Sk (€95). Breakfast & VAT included. City tax 30Sk (€0.80) extra.

Film Hotel Vysoká ulica 27; ☏ 02 5293 1600; f 02 5292 1394; e reception@filmhotel.sk; www.filmhotel.sk [2 E3]

T̲ 9 along Obchodná

An elegant town house situated at the far end of Obchodná, the main shopping street leading northeast out of town. Aside from bumping into the occasional giant Oscar statue or walking over star names on the tiled floor, the experience is not really as tacky as it sounds. Rooms are comfortable and spacious and the building is quite elegant from the outside apart from the neon. Rooms are named after film stars: the deluxe ones are Marilyn Monroe, Brigitte Bardot and Robert De Niro; classic rooms are Marlon Brando and Al Pacino while Messrs Cruise, Hanks, Gere, Pitt, Willis, Gibson and DiCaprio along with Julia Roberts are merely 'standard'…what would their agents say? It's all a bit gimmicky but, hey, if you come for a stag weekend and then go home and tell your mates you spent the night in Julia Roberts's room, it's not such a big porky. Film restaurant continues in the same cinematic vein. 13 rooms. Deluxe sgl 2,500Sk (€64), dbl 3,200Sk (€82), standard sgl 2,200Sk (€57), dbl 2,700Sk (€69), classic sgl 1,500Sk (€39), dbl 2,000Sk (€51). Breakfast is 150Sk (€4) a day extra. Euro prices may vary according to exchange rates.

Hotel Blue Riazanska 38; ☎ 02 4949 2222; f 02 4949 2555; e recepcia@hotelblue.sk; www.hotelblue.sk
T̄ 2, 4, 6; B̄ 50; N̄B̄ 514
Situated near the Polus Center shopping mall, out in the northeastern suburbs of town, Chelsea fans will feel right at home amongst all that royal blue décor. The only other colour is white which gives a clean, smart and slightly nautical effect. Hotel Blue is geared towards business travellers and those arriving by car. Air-conditioned rooms have widescreen TVs and free internet access. A small restaurant serves international cuisine. 24 rooms (22 business dbls, 2 business apts). Business dbl Mon–Thu 3,590Sk (€92), Fri–Sun 2,900Sk (€75), business apt Mon–Thu 8,500Sk (€219) Fri–Sun 5,900Sk (€152). À la carte breakfast included. City tax 30Sk (€0.80) extra.

Hotel Ibis Bratislava Centrum Zámocká 38; ☎ 02 5929 2000; f 02 5929 2111; e h3566@accor-hotels.com; www.ibis-bratislava.sk [1 A2]
T̄ 5, 9, 12; B̄ 31, 39, 81, 83, 84, 93, 94, 131, 180; N̄B̄ 503, 504, 506, 507, 508
Situated right next to the tram tunnel under Castle Hill, the Hotel Ibis has a convenient location and the tram noise is not too disturbing. Near to the Old Town and the castle,

Hotels

rooms are simple and fairly featureless but with good, smart bathrooms. Rather impersonal surroundings, run by the French Accor chain the hotel has the chain's 15-minute guarantee: if a problem caused by the hotel is not resolved within 15 minutes, that night's accommodation is free. Two rooms equipped for disabled visitors. Also has a business corner, restaurant and bar. 120 rooms. Dbl €72 (€65 at weekends). Expensive breakfast (310Sk/€8) not included.

Hotel Incheba Viedenská cesta 7; ☎ 02 6727 2000; f 02 6727 2542; e hotel@incheba.sk; www.incheba.sk [4 C8]
Located next to the Bratislava exhibition centre on the Petržalka side of the Danube, and amazingly only five minutes by car from the Austrian border. The tower block building is part of a grotesque concrete complex that defaces the cityscape view from Castle Hill. Convenient for those attending one of the multitude of conventions or exhibitions at the Incheba (pronounced with the 'ch' like that in the Scottish 'loch') centre next door, but otherwise nothing to write home about. Fitness room, sauna, squash courts. 136 beds. Higher prices during exhibitions; sgl 1,700Sk (€44), dbl 2,000Sk (€51), apts 2,500Sk (€64), family room 3,240Sk (€83) including VAT. Breakfast (150Sk/€4) not included. City tax 30Sk (€0.80) extra.

Hotel Kyjev Rajská 2; ☎ 2 5964 1111; f 02 5292 6820; e rezervacia@kyjev-hotel.sk, www.kyjev-hotel.sk [1 E1, 3 F4]
Ⓣ 4, 6, 11, 14
Sky-rise 1960s hotel located just behind the Tesco supermarket. It is one of the few cheaper hotels in such a central location. In the communist era, it was popular with visiting dignitaries and businessmen and the atmosphere of those days still lingers in the

décor, although service has greatly improved as the receptionists are too charming and welcoming to maintain a grim KGB ambience. It's a little basic, but a good choice for bargain hunters especially if you don't mind going without a TV, as you get a lower rate. All rooms have en-suite bathroom and toilet and excellent views from rooms nearer the top of the 15 storeys. The restaurant is good but the elevators are not for the faint-hearted, being a little old and cranky. Suitable for Soviet nostalgists and those on a tight budget. 380 beds. A two-tier price system for 'with TV' and 'without TV'. With TV, sgl 2,000Sk (€51), dbl 2,600Sk (€69), triples 3,400Sk (€87). Without TV, sgl 1,600Sk (€41), dbl 2,000Sk (€51), triple 2,800Sk (€72). Breakfast included.

Hotel Sorea Kralovske udolie 6; ☏ 02 5441 4442; f 02 5441 1017; e hotel@sorea.sk; www.sorea.sk

B̄ 29, 30, 31, 39; T̄ 1, 4, 5, 9, 12; N̄B̄ 502, 503, 504; T̄ 1 to PKO (Park Kultury) stop, cross street and walk up steps for 50m

A modern building situated in a green, hilly area out to the west of town, overlooking the Danube. Hotel Sorea is owned by the Slovak labour unions so you are likely to bump into troops of Slovak pensioners enjoying a hefty discount. It's another hotel with a retro-commie chic; check out the mirrored bar and ceiling in the lobby. Rooms are simple with en-suite facilities. Internet available. Restaurant, day bar and Hubert night bar. Some difficulties with staff's command of English. 65 rooms. Economy dbl 1,600Sk (€41), standard dbl 1,960Sk (€50), business dbl 2,600Sk (€69). Breakfast à la carte 160Sk (€4), buffet 200Sk (€5) not included. City tax 30Sk (€0.80) extra.

Hotels

Hotel Tatra Námestie 1. mája 5; ☏ 02 5927 2111; f 02 5927 2135;
e recepcia@hoteltatra.sk; www.hoteltatra.sk [2 E3]
$\underline{B}$ 34, 81, 83, 84, 93, 180; $\underline{TB}$ 203, 206, 207, 208, 212; $\underline{NB}$ 503, 504, 506, 507, 508, 510, 511, 512, 513, 515, 516

Tatra opened in the 1930s but was recently reconstructed. The hotel is located near the centre of town in a complex that houses a cinema and a dance club. Good value, all new and just along the road from the Crowne Plaza. The upholstery is very lurid in a strange shade of green, but otherwise recommended. Good restaurant, Old Bratislava, and tasty breakfasts. Small fitness room with sauna and whirlpool. Business centre with internet facilities. Rooms have TV with free video channels and free minibar. 37 standard sgl €88, 40 standard dbl €108, 5 luxury dbl €121, 4 suites €173, extra bed €25. Breakfast, City tax and 19% VAT included.

Two-star

Hotels marked with two stars often offer both decent accommodation and good value for money but apart from Hotel Kyjev (two-star if you go for a room without a TV; for information see the three-star hotel list), which is the best for location, the others are usually further out from the centre.

Two-star hotels have en-suite rooms with bath and/or shower, television, radio and sometimes a fridge.

Hotel Remy Stará Vajnorská cesta 37/a, near Zlaté Piesky lake resort; ☏ 02 4445 5063; f 02 4425 7026; e info@remy.sk; www.remy.sk

$\overline{T}$ 2, 4, to Zlaté Piesky terminus; $\overline{B}$ 53, 56, 65; $\overline{NB}$ 514

Remy is a basic hotel, situated out by the Zlaté Piesky lake. Apart from the lake resort the area unfortunately is dominated by industry and main roads so not too restful. Simple, but clean rooms have en-suite facilities, satellite TV, radio and telephone. Internet access at the 24-hour reception for 100Sk (€2.60) an hour. 46 dbl rooms and 1 dbl with facilities for disabled visitors. Sgl €29, dbl €33, breakfast from €1.25.

Hotel Turist Ondravská 5; ☎ 02 5541 0508; f 02 5557 3180; e hotel@turist.sk; www.turisk.sk

$\overline{B}$ 39, 53, 61, 63, 68, 74, 75, 78, 198; $\overline{TB}$ 204, 205; $\overline{NB}$ 512, 513

Located about 3km northeast of the centre, heading for the airport and just off Trnavská cesta, in the Ružinov district, close to both ice hockey stadiums. Turist is an old-style bargain hotel, with not much to offer except price and ice hockey. Rooms are clean with en-suite facilities and all have a small balcony. However, the showers are designed in such a way that the bathroom always gets flooded during ablutions. Satellite TV in every room and most rooms have a fridge and phone. Good for groups. Restaurant is nothing special. 99 rooms. Sgl 1,080Sk (€28), dbl 1,340Sk (€34). Breakfast (60–90Sk/€1.50–2.30) not included.

One-star

Of the one-star hotels situated near enough to town, only Zvárač merits a mention. It has no restaurant or breakfast, but there are communal kitchens on the third and fourth floors, so it would suit those used to hostel accommodation. Some rooms have bathroom and toilet shared between two rooms.

Hotels

Zvárač Pionierska 17; ☏ 02 4924 6600; f 02 4924 6545; e hotel@vuz.sk; www.vuz.sk
Ⓣ 3, 5, 7, 11; Ⓑ 50, 51; N̲B̲ 515; Ⓣ 3 *to Pionerska*

Situated north of the centre, in a more industrial part of town, the name 'Zvárač' means 'welder' and the hotel is part of the Welding Research Institute. If metalworking is your hobby, you'll be right at home, but otherwise this hotel is clean and cheap but a little far from town. Zvárač retains some of the old socialist workers' or students' hostel-style facilities and some rooms have a shared shower and toilet in a connecting passage between two rooms, which Zvárač unintentionally refers to as 'cells'. There is also a shared kitchenette on the third and fourth floors. No restaurant or breakfast facilities. The better rooms have been reconstructed and have TV, radio and fridge. Good for students. Sgl 850–900Sk, dbl 850–1,350Sk. Price includes 19% VAT but 15Sk City tax per person per night is extra.

PENSIONS AND PRIVATE APARTMENTS/ROOMS
Pensions

Pensions are popular with many travellers as they are often smaller and cheaper than regular hotels and have a family atmosphere missing in a big international venue. The selection listed are all either in the centre or within easy walking distance. Some are more basic, others quite luxurious. All provide clean, modern rooms with en-suite bathroom and/or shower. Some have restaurants attached which can hold their own against the best in town.

Accommodation

Private apartments

There are lot of both short-term and long-term apartments available.

BKIS (*Klobučnícka 2*) has a list of the best and can suggest places to stay if you want to do your own cooking and cleaning. Most of them are situated in the Old Town and equipped with cable television, phone, washing machine, oven or microwave. Some of them also provide internet access.

Apartment Hotel Residence Šulekova Šulekova 20; ✆ 02 54419383; f 02 5441 9388; e info@mamaisonresidences.com; www.mamaisonresidences.com [2 A2]

TB *203, 205, 208;* NB *516;* TB *208 from Hodžovo námestie to the terminus*

Located in a quiet residential street, not far from Hotel Antares, this apartment block is also four star and offers 9 different layouts and varying sizes, from the standard 33m² to the deluxe 76m². Šulekova is ideal for business travellers or relocating executives, but also for families who want self-catering. The apartments are tastefully furnished with parquet floors and beige curtains, livened up with bright, colourful and fully equipped kitchens. Free high-speed internet in all apartments and free WiFi internet in the lobby and meeting room. Guarded parking places available on request. 32 apts. Standard apt €143 (daily), €107 (weekly), €78 (monthly), business apt €179 (daily), €131 (weekly), €90 (monthly), deluxe dbl €393 (daily), €286 (weekly), €236 (monthly). Breakfast €9 extra. City tax extra.

Arcus Moskovská 5; ✆ 02 5557 2522; f 02 5557 6750; e bratislava@hotelarcus.sk; www.hotelarcus.sk [3 H2]

T *1, 4, 5, 6, 9, 11, 14 from Kamenné námestie to Americké námestie*

Intimate, friendly pension situated just northeast of the charming Medical Gardens (Medická záhrada), within walking distance of the Old Town. Each room has unique character and bathrooms vary to suit taste. Long-term guests get separate kitchen and terrace. TV, radio, minibar, telephone and internet possibilities. Sgl 1,400Sk (€37), dbl 2,600Sk (€69). Breakfast included.

Caribic's Žižkova 1/A, ☎ 02 5441 8334; f 02 5442 8333; e caribics@stonline.sk; www.caribics.sk [4 A6]

Caribic's is situated in the old fishing quarter of town, out to the west of the centre, between the base of Castle Hill and the Danube. The pension has a superb fish restaurant with maritime décor, brickwork and oyster shells. The building is partly thatched, an unusual feature for houses by the Danube. It used to share the premises with the Rybársky Cech restaurant, in a historic rococo fisherman's lodge built in 1759–60 by N Danko. The Rybársky Cech closed three years ago and now the premises is occupied by an advertising agency, OMD. The pension would make an excellent place to stay for honeymooners, as it is a little away from the bustle of the centre and very romantic. Two sgls 950Sk, four dbls 1,800Sk, one apt for four 2,900Sk. Breakfast included.

Castle Club Bed & Breakfast Zámocké schody 4; ☎/f 02 5464 1472; e castleclub@stonline.sk [4 B6] Part of the *Bratislava Business Journal* group of services; m 0903 264 357 or 0903 185 900

B̲ 29, 30, 31, 37, 39, 70, 71, 80, 81, 83, 90, 91, 93; T̲ 1, 4, 5, 9, 12; N̲B̲ 503, 504, 506, 507, 508

The pension is located on Castle Hill, a brief (albeit steep) walk of about five minutes from the centre of the Old Town. Three types of rooms: sgl, triple (dbl and twin bed) and a large attic bedroom with two dbl beds. Big brown old-fashioned ceramic stove heater in living room and parquet throughout. Attic four-bed room is equipped with a satellite TV, internet access and has a separate bathroom with a shower and a toilet. Hairdryer is provided in all rooms. Not suitable for people with disabilities or older people unable to walk up the hill. 10% discount is provided for visits over five days. Laundry service is available on request. The Castle Club can organise bed and breakfast accommodation in central locations of Bratislava for €15 a night. Pension dbl €50, triple €60, attic €80. Breakfast included.

Chez David Zámocká 13; ☏ 02 5441 3824; f 02 5441 2642; e recepcia@chezdavid.sk; www.chezdavid.sk [1 A2, 4 B5]
Plush kosher pension located on a hill leading north away from the castle quarter. The building's exterior is not very attractive, but the interior is tastefully furnished and all rooms are elegant with en-suite facilities. An added bonus is the superb kosher restaurant within the building. Sgl €62, dbl €88, suites €130, weekend sgl €54, weekend dbl €78. Breakfast included. City tax 15Sk a night.

Gremium Gorkého 10; ☏ 02 5413 1025; f 02 5443 0653; e cherrytour@mail.pvt.sk; www.gremium.sk [1 D3, 4 E5]
T̲ 1, 4, 11, 12, 14
Situated above the Gremium pub and popular sports bar, running for 14 years. Open daily 08.30–midnight (breakfast for guests upstairs, but bar opens at 11.00). Centrally located, clean with extremely basic en-suite bathrooms. The rooms are furnished in a simple, cosy

and modest style and have functional en-suite shower facilities and toilet. Good for young people, sports fans etc. Internet phone line available for dial-up connection. Sport café/restaurant with big screen and sports-betting in the building. Restaurant serves various cuisines including Slovak, Italian, American and Mexican. Five rooms. Sgl 950Sk (€24), dbl 1,850Sk (€48), twins 1,650Sk (€42). Breakfast extra.

HOSTELS

Quite a few hostels are open only in the summer as they are located in student dormitories. Ask at BKIS for a list of summer youth hostels (N Belojanisa, Nešporák, Domov Mládeže, Družba, Jura Hronica, Mlada Garda, Mladosť, STU, Svoradov).

Downtown Hostel Backpacker's Panenska 31; ☎ 02 5464 1191; e info@backpackers.sk; www.backpackers.sk [2 C3]

$\overline{\text{B}}$ 34, 81, 83, 84, 93; $\overline{\text{T}}$ 203, 205, 206, 208, 212; $\overline{\text{NB}}$ 503, 504, 506, 507, 508, 510, 511, 512, 513, 515, 516

Located near the Presidential Palace in a historic building, Downtown provides clean, modern rooms and friendly staff. Kitchen, laundry and non-stop internet access available. The hostel offers dorm rooms and a limited number of private rooms. The bathroom and toilet facilities for both types of rooms are shared and located in the hallway. The hostel does provide bed linen but does not provide towels. A member of the Hostelling International (HI) network thus offering a 10% discount for HI card holders. Suitable for backpackers and other young travellers, especially on account of the shared bathroom facilities. Other facilities: laundry, bar, kitchen, summer garden (patio). Internet access available non-stop. Smoking is not allowed in the hostel rooms. 44 beds. Dorms €13–15, dbl €21–24.

Gabriel's Backpacker Paulíniho 1; m 0903 783 333; e gabrielslovak@e-zones.sk; http://gabriel.hostelslovakia.net [1 C4, 4 D6]
Formerly Hostel Gabriel, good location between Hviezdoslavovo námestie and the river Danube. Situated in a residential house, open all year round, no curfew, shared kitchen. Dorm bed 600Sk (€15), private dbl loft 600Sk (€15), private triple 800Sk (€20), private room for four 700Sk (€18).

Patio Hostel Špitálska 35; ☏ 02 5292 5797; e booking@patiohostel.com; www.patiohostel.com [3 G3]
T̄ 4, 6, 7, 11, 14, 17; T̄B̄ 202
Situated on the road leading from Tesco up to the Medical Garden, Patio is a new hostel with accommodation in dbl-, triple-, four- and eight-bedded dorm rooms. Bed linen provided. Free internet access, laundry, TV room and friendly staff. Kitchen is fully equipped on each floor with cutlery and pans. The bathroom and toilet facilities for all rooms are shared and located on each floor. Suitable for backpackers and young travellers, on account of the shared bathroom facilities. 57 beds (16 rooms). Twin/dbl 780Sk (€20) Sun–Thu, 830Sk (€21) Fri–Sat, triple 680Sk (€17) Sun–Thu, 730Sk (€17) Fri–Sat, 4-bed room 630Sk (€16) Sun–Thu, 680Sk (€17) Fri–Sat, 8-bed dorm 530SK (€14) Sun–Thu, 580Sk (€15)

Hostels

Fri–Sat. Local tax 30Sk (€0.80) included. Students under 25, disabled and elderly are exempt from this tax.

Spirit Vančurova 1; ☏ 02 5465 2711; e info@hotelspirit.sk; www.hotelspirit.sk
T̄ 1 from town centre; B̄ 210 from main bus station, 61 from airport
Welcoming yet bizarre hostel-cum-hotel located behind the railway station. The building is painted in bright colours both inside and out and aims to help visitors achieve certain fitness and spiritual health goals during their stay. Each guest receives a complimentary nutrition supplement according to their current health conditions. Guests can also spend time in a relaxation/regeneration pyramid for 30Sk (€0.80) an hour. 20 rooms. Sgl 1,500Sk (€39), dbl 1,830Sk (€47), triples 2,360Sk (€61), 4-bed room 2,835Sk (€73), luxury apt 4,100Sk (€105), dorm bed 800Sk (€21). One meal a day included.

CAMPING
Autocamp Zlaté Piesky Senecká cesta 2; ☏ 02 4425 7373, e kempi@netax.sk; www.intercamp.sk
T̄ 2, 4 to Zlaté Piesky terminus
Intercamp and Autocamp Zlaté Piesky are two campsites at the 54ha lake resort. Zlaté Piesky is a large lake outside the centre where small cabins can be rented. The site has a capacity for 300 pitches for tents and trailers; 40 chalets, simply equipped, can sleep up to 160 people. The bungalows have private shower, kitchen and small fridge. The apartments sleep up to four, with separate bedroom, family room and equipped kitchen area, also TV, private shower, own parking

place and picnic area. The beach can hold 15,000 people and water bicycles can be hired. There is also water tobogganing, mini-golf, table tennis, beach volleyball, street basketball and children's play area. Reception is open daily between 08.00 and 22.00 during low season and 24 hours during high season (Jul–Aug). A tourist information centre is found next to reception. Open daily during summer season 08.00–18.00 for sale of tram tickets, stamps, maps, newspapers and magazines. At Zlaté Piesky there are two restaurants, 15 buffet stalls and an on-site shop with basic foodstuffs and fresh vegetables and fruit. Chalet with fridge 700–890Sk (€18–23), bungalow 1,030Sk (€26), apt (2+2) 1,900Sk (€49), Stamo (chalet for 10 people) 2,100Sk (€54), car parking 50Sk (€1.30). Camping: adult 90Sk (€2.30), child 55Sk (€1.40), car 70Sk (€1.80), camper 160Sk (€4.10), caravan 110Sk (€2.80), tent (3+) 70Sk (€1.80), tent (2+) 55Sk (€1.40), tax 30Sk (€0.80). Discount after 8 days 10%, after 14 days 15%.

6 Eating and drinking

Láska ide cez žalúdok (Love goes through the stomach)

Slovak cuisine is a mélange of central European influences, taking a bit of everything from its neighbours: goulash from the Magyars, strudels from the Austrians, home-kneaded dumplings from the Germans.

Slovak chefs are expertly trained in the meat, potato and cabbage school of cooking, and finding something less heavy will involve hunting down a restaurant with an international menu, or at least one that does lighter versions of the sturdy traditional dishes.

A hundred years ago, most Slovaks lived on and from the land and robust peasant cooking still dominates the national psyche. This is the land of cabbage, caraway seeds, cheese, wheat flour, potatoes and endless variations on the theme of pork. However, after a day hiking through the High Tatras or visiting castle ruins, such hearty fare can be just the thing.

After 1,000 years under Magyar domination and 40 years of communism, Slovakia's restaurant culture remains in its infancy, although in Bratislava they are catching on quickly. This guide to restaurants offers a selection of both traditional and international places to try the local dishes or stick with something you know.

FOOD

Breakfast (*raňajky*) at home is bread with butter, cheese, ham, sausage, eggs, peppers and tomatoes, jam and yoghurt, washed down with tea with lemon or strong coffee. Some new cafés in Bratislava serve pastries or local versions of croissants (*lúpačky*). On the run, some people nibble on frankfurters (*párky*) and crescent rolls at the buffet on the way to work, followed by elevenses early at 10.00.

To see how Slovaks **snack**, visit the Main Market (Stará Trznica) on Námestie SNP, where there is a variety of stalls offering pies (*buchty*), potato pancakes (*lokša*) with savoury fillings such as cabbage, poppyseed or garlic, giant deep-fried doughnuts (*langoše*) topped with sour cream or grated cheese. There are also pancakes (*palacinky*) with a choice of 50 fillings. The market also has a wine bar, more proletarian than Knightsbridge in character and busy with the freshly drawn draughts of grape juice from early morning onwards.

Lunch (*obed*) is the main meal of the day, a serious event of soup, followed by a substantial main course and dessert. Unless they eat out, Slovaks' **dinner** (*večera*) is a bit like breakfast, a do-it-yourself affair with bread and cold meats, cheeses and pickles.

Back to the main event – *obed*. This should begin with a soup (*polievka*), although some locals might claim that meals actually begin with a shot of slivovica (plum brandy). Slovak cooking is so robust that appetisers (*predjedlá*) are rarely necessary. For those with a healthy appetite, a slice of ham rolled around horseradish cream

Food

(*šunková rolka s chrenovou penou*) could fill a gap. The tangy fresh sheep's cheese (*bryndza*) or raw onions and lard sometimes appears on simpler menus as a beer accompaniment, served with bread (*chlieb*), a Slovak staple. Soups are usually thick; no watery gruel here. Cabbage soup (*kapustnica*) is one of the best-known soups, livened up with smoked pork, cream, mushrooms and sometimes plums. Bean soup (*fazuľová polievka*) is another hearty concoction with more smoked pork knuckle to give bite.

Salads (*šaláty*) are often created from the ubiquitous cabbage, while the lettuce and tomato kind may be more limp.

Magyar neighbours gave Slovaks goulash (*guláš*), a stew with meat (pork, beef, or both), potatoes and carrots, laced with onions, caraway seeds and paprika. The Viennese lent their schnitzels and the Istrian coast offered a delicious stew of smoked pork and sauerkraut.

The best-known dish is *bryndzové halušky* (also known in Hungary as *sztrapácska*), boiled gnocchi-sized dumplings made of potato dough and served with tangy sheep's cheese and topped with bacon cubes. It's excellent for soaking up the alcohol after an evening of beer-sampling, but those watching their cholesterol or waistline should not risk it more than once a week. This dish is quite often served to vegetarians, as some older Slovaks don't grasp the concept of not eating meat, and anyway bacon fat isn't meat, is it?

On many menus, the only veggie option is fried cheese (*vyprážaný syr*) with chips (*hranolky*) and tartare sauce. Personally, I put on pounds when living in Brno during

MARKET VALUES

If all those dumplings are getting you down and you hanker for some fresh fruit, check out the markets — here are some ideas:

Stará Tržnica Main market entrance on Námestie SNP, and a little shop called Olivy selling dried fruit and nuts, weighed out

Tržnica Huge market at Trnavské mýto

Lekareň Many pharmacies sell reasonably priced vitamins.

Obchodná A girl with a stall by bus stop selling dried fruit and nuts, sold by weight

Corn on the cob, jacket potatoes, chestnuts at little stall opposite McDonald's on **Hviezdoslavovo námestie**

my veggie days on an artery-clogging diet of fried cheese and beer.

Lečo is eaten throughout the region. It's a delicious concoction of tomatoes, peppers and onions, a kind of poor man's ratatouille. It can be supplemented with chopped frankfurters, a stirred-in raw egg or boiled rice.

Slovak main dishes tend to be heavily based on meat (*mäso*). Pork (*bravčové*) is king here. It comes as ribs (*rebierko*), chops (*karé* or *rezy*) or steak (*roštenka*). A slab

Food

SLOVAK GRAPE VARIETIES

Slovak winemaking history dates back to the 7th century BC when Celts grew vines on the hilly land northeast of Bratislava. The continental climate makes Slovakia, like Hungary, ideal for producing fruity whites (favoured by German and Austrian drinkers) and robust reds. It's still almost impossible to find Slovenské vino outside Slovakia but pop into Tesco or Delvita and you'll be amazed first by the price (avg 200Sk/£4 a bottle) then pleasantly stunned by the quality. The white wine is more reliable than the red and the Tokaj could be taken home as an excellent gift to sweeten up your mother-in-law. To be sure of getting something drinkable, stick to wines above 200Sk.

Words to look for on the label are *červené* (red), *biele* (white), *ružové* (rosé), *suché* (dry), *sladké* (sweet), *akostné* (quality), *výber* (choice) and *vina s prívlastkom* (wine with a special attribute). www.wineshop.sk sells Slovak wine online.

The whites

Chardonnay This French variety is a popular grape in Slovakia

Devín A new full-bodied, acidic variety developed by Slovak enologists

Müller-Thurgau The most widely planted white grape in Slovakia (and Germany). Created by Dr Hermann Müller-Thurgau in 1882 from two strains of Riesling.

Pálava As in 'What a palaver'? Another new variety developed in the Czech Republic, it's a cross between Tramín and Müller-Thurgau.

Rizling Rýnsky German Riesling, with crisp, fruity finish

Rizling Vlašský Welschriesling from the Champagne region of France

Rulandské Biele French Pinot Blanc with good acids

Sauvignon (Blanc) French variety popular with Slovak winemakers

Tramín Gewürztraminer and very flowery

Tokaj These grapes are normally associated with Hungary, but after the Trianon treaty some got left in Slovakia when the borders were drawn up. It's a sweet dessert wine like a Sauterne.

The reds

Alibernet Cabernet Sauvignon hybrid

Frankovka Modrá Popular on the wine route, you can find some in Pezinok

Modrý Portugal Blauer Portugueser is lighter than most

Neronet Like Alibernet it's a Cab hybrid

Rulandské Modré Pinot Noir, an ingredient of Burgundy

Svätovavrinecké French St Lawrence with good body

of pork is quite often stuffed with a ham and/or cheese.

Fried, grilled or roast poultry (*hydina*) is popular, with turkey (*morka*) and chicken (*kurča*) leading the way. Beef (*hovädzie*) appears on many menus but is more expensive than the other meats. Freshwater fish, such as carp (*kapor*) and trout (*pstruh*), from local rivers can be bony but tasty. Restaurant menus give a base price for 150g then add on a charge for every 10g over. When ordering fish, tell the waiter if you only want a little fishy on your dishy. Carp is a traditional Christmas Eve dish throughout the Slav world, which can be simply fried (*vyprážaný*), grilled (*na rošte*), or served with nuts (*s orechami*) or heaps of garlic (*s cesnakom*).

After selecting a main course, you then have to choose a side dish (*príloha*): potatoes (*zemiaky*), rice (*ryža*) or an unenthusiastic portion of deep-frozen veg. Slovak restaurants charge extra for side dishes, and waiters are disturbed if you don't order one. The potatoes are always reliable and arrive baked (*zapekané zemiaky*), boiled (*varené zemiaky*), mashed (*zemiaková kaša*) or fried (*opekané zemiaky*). Chips or French fries (*hranolky*) are everywhere.

The star of dessert (*dezert*) menus is the pancake (*palacinky*). These have sweet fillings: chocolate (*s čokoládou*), jam (*s džemom*) or a ricotta-esque cheese (*s tvarohom*). Sweetened noodles (*rezance*) topped with poppy seeds and melted butter are also popular. Slovaks love cakes and pastries. See the *Cafés and tearooms* section for a few pointers.

DRINK

Slovak mineral water (*minerálna voda*) is delicious and contains many life-enhancing properties. Also popular are soft drinks like *kofola* (Czech cola) that's mixed with soda water and often available on draught in half-litre mugs. *Vinea* is a refreshing grape juice drink sold in tall green bottles and local fruit juices are excellent.

For centuries under Hungarian rule, the peasant population had little access to wine (*vino*) which went to nobles throughout the kingdom, although the lower-quality stuff did serve as an everyday drink in wine-producing areas. Beer (*pivo*), the beverage of the rising burgher class, cost too much for most peasants to buy, and it was illegal to make it without a licence from the king.

Slovaks used to distil at home the produce from their orchards, creating the famous, fiery slivovica (plum brandy), and similar paint-stripping brews from pears, cherries and apricots. Borovička is made from juniper berries and tastes a bit like gin. It's said to be the best cure for a cold. Demänovka is another bittersweet herbal liqueur while the cinnamony Becherovka is Czech but also worth a try.

A honey wine, Medovina, used to be made in nearly every village home. This custom has dwindled although most villages still have at least one beekeeper. This mead-like drink is still served hot at Bratislava Christmas market.

RESTAURANTS

Many restaurants place copies of the **menu** by the front door on the outside wall, so you can get an idea of the food and the prices before you venture in. This is not

SLOVAK BEER

I've mentioned only the most frequently encountered beers. Some pubs will have more varieties. Look out for *svetlé* (light, lager), *tmavé pivo* (dark beer), *výčapné pivo* (draught/on tap beer); www.pivo.sk is good but only if your language skills are as good as your beer-drinking capacity.

Corgoň Produced by Heineken

Gambrinus Made by Šariš

Kelt Produced by Heineken

Kozel Light beer

Martiner Original Produced by Heineken

Šariš (light beer and *tmavé* – dark) Brewed in Velký Šariš near Prešov in eastern Slovakia

Smädný Mních (Thirsty Monk) Made by Šariš

Stein (light beer and *tmavé* – dark)

Topvar (light, Millennium and *tmavé* – dark)

Zlatý Bažant (Golden Pheasant) (light beer and *tmavé* – dark) Started in 1968 in Hurbanovo, near Komárno, as a state-owned enterprise supplying beer to western Slovakia; bought by Heineken in 1995

compulsory as in Budapest, but because of a 'good local habit' to be helpful. It also gives restaurants the chance of showing their wares in the hope of tempting visitors to enter. Big-name restaurants like Le Monde don't have to do it, as they rely on their considerable reputation.

All restaurants in Bratislava are required by law to issue a printed **receipt** from the electronic cash register, so if you have any concerns over the bill, make sure you get one.

Bratislava Old Town is wall-to-wall eat-out city with cafés, bars, cocktail venues, restaurants, self-service canteens, stand-up buffet stalls – you're totally spoilt. Slovak, international, Mediterranean, Mexican, Japanese, there's a great choice and it's doubtful that you'll need to book, apart from at the 'place of the month', as if your intended eaterie is full, just totter two yards along the pavement and you'll find another option.

Reservations

Major credit cards are usually accepted, but check first, before launching into the chateaubriand steak for two and champagne supper.

The sections on restaurants, cafés and pubs have all been divided into two main districts: **Old Town and Castle District** and **Beyond the Old Town gates, Centrum and further afield.** Only occasionally will you have to take a taxi to your choice of chow venue, as the majority can be reached on foot.

Restaurants

WHERE TO NOSH

In Slovakia, eating and drinking venues announce themselves with words that may not be immediately recognisable. Apart from '*reštaurácia*' and '*bufet*', the signs on establishments can leave visitors confused. Here is an explanation of some of the places to check out for food and drink.

Reštaurácia restaurant
Jedeleň canteen
Bufet stand-up noshing venue
Cukráreň patisserie (from the word 'cukor' – sugar)
Pivaren/pivnica beer hall
Vinareň wine tavern (literally 'wine cellar')
Kavárieň coffee house
Koliba rustic country restaurant offering grilled meats (literally 'a hut')
Krčma pub

Old Town and Castle District

Archa Uršulínska 6; ☏ 02 5443 0865; www.archacafe.sk [1 C2]
Archa attracts a young crowd with its blue-and-red décor, groovy taste in music and varied international menu. Good pasta dishes (120Sk), salads (99Sk) and the chance to top it off

with 'hot love' (*horúca láska*) – hot raspberries with caramel, rum and vanilla ice cream (79Sk for 200g). Serves good coffee and has outdoor seating in summer. Mains 99–149Sk (avg 120Sk). *Open Mon–Fri 09.00–midnight, Sat–Sun 10.00–midnight.*

Corrida de Toros Laurinská 7; ☎ 02 5443 5741 [1 C2]
Spanish restaurant with a summer terrace. Inside, the yellowing 'distressed' walls, peeling bullfight posters and wrought-iron staircase give good atmosphere. The grilled trout is delicious but the 'English vegetables' (*anglická zelinina*) is a nightmare of carrot cubes straight out of the deep freeze and barely thawed cauliflower. Credit cards accepted. Mains 60–330Sk (avg 200Sk). *Open Sun–Thu 09.00–midnight, Fri–Sat 09.00–03.00.*

Divesta Laurinská 8 [1 C3]
In the land where pork is king, the longest lunch queues stretch right out of this veggie bistro and down Laurinská. Good choice of dishes, a lot of soya chunks, menu in English as well. Plain and simple vegetarian lunch spot, with a short list of salads and soya-based main dishes. *Open Mon–Fri 11.00–15.00.*

Gazdovsky Dvor Zelená 5; ☎ 02 5443 1818; www.perugia.sk [1 B3]
The name translates as 'homestead's courtyard' although they call it 'farmyard' which has a certain odour. Part of the Hotel Perugia and offering Hungarian–Slovak country cuisine in a rustic barn setting. Strings of peppers and garlic dangle from the exposed beams. Mains 140–300Sk (avg 200Sk). *Open Mon–Fri 07.00–23.00, Sat–Sun 08.00–23.00.*

Hacienda Mexicana Sedlárska 6; ☎ 02 5464 2103; www.mexicana.sk [1 B3]
Faux Mexican cantina situated above El Diablo and slap bang next to Dubliners. Part of a

Czech chain, it does steaks, salads, pasta, paella and all the Mexican favourites. The Aztec murals are getting a bit dowdy, but the grub is always reliable. Mains 149–319Sk (avg 240Sk). Credit cards accepted. *Open daily 11.30–midnight.*

Hradná vináreň Námestie A Dubčeka 1; ↘ 02 5934 1358 [1 A3]
Smart restaurant and wine bar in the castle grounds, with smashing view of the Old Town and the Danube. Favourite expat grazing ground, Slovak specialities include an interesting game goulash. Mains 260–600Sk (avg 350Sk). *Open daily 11.00–23.00.*

Ludwig Restaurant Ventúrska 7; ↘ 02 5464 8284; www.ludwig.sk [1 B3]
An elegant restaurant and café with creamy upholstery and white arches, set back from the street, in one of Bratislava's oldest buildings. Separate non-smoking area. French and Slovak cuisine with some interesting ostrich dishes. Divine pumpkin soup with chestnuts (140Sk). Mains 250–550Sk (avg 400Sk). *Open daily 11.00–midnight.*

Medusa Michalská 21; ↘ 02 5464 7344 [1 B2]
Medusa subtitles itself as 'pasta bar and restaurant' and there is an excellent choice of Italian dishes in this chic clubby space. Quesadillas, quiches and baguettes at very reasonable prices. Gorgeous desserts, cocktails and not a snake-haired maiden in sight. Mains 119–390Sk (avg 200Sk). *Open Mon–Thu 11.00–01.00, Fri–Sat 11.00–03.00, Sun 11.00–midnight.*

Mezzo Mezzo Rybárska brána 9; ↘ 02 5443 4393; www.mezzo.sk [1 C3]
The subtler Mezzo Mezzo lurks just behind a brash Mcburger bar at Fisherman's Gate

Eating and drinking

(Rybárska brána) and offers quality dishes in a snazzy setting. Well situated for a dinner before or after a performance at the National Theatre or the Reduta. Also an excellent breakfast venue with a full English (avg 300Sk). Credit cards accepted. Mains 320–830Sk (avg 540Sk). *Open Mon–Fri 08.00–01.00, Sat–Sun 09.00–01.00.*

Modra Hviezda Beblavého 14; ☏ 02 5443 2747; www.modrahviezda.sk [1 A3]
The 'blue star' restaurant en route to the castle serving Slovak and Hungarian specialities in a stable setting in an 18th-century late Baroque building with a history; allegedly the revolutionary poet Sándor Petôfi used to come here for the delicious Bencze cabbage, which you can still try today. Mains 100–250Sk (avg 180Sk). *Open daily 11.30–23.00.*

Paparazzi Laurinská 1; ☏ 02 5464 7971; www.paparazzi.sk [1 C3]
A 19th-century neo-Classical building contains a chic Italian restaurant with pricey dishes, cocktails and a hip, eye-catching crowd. To accentuate the paparazzi theme, creepy pictures of Bono and Naomi Campbell are blown up in the window; Bono appears to have Naomi in a headlock. Outside, a statue of a photographer sneaks a picture from around a corner with a long telephoto lens. Mains 480–680Sk (avg 580Sk). *Open daily 10.00–01.00.*

Prašná Bašta Zámočnícka 11; ☏ 02 5443 4957; www.prasnabasta.sk [1 B/C2]
Quiet courtyard and restful, cosy interior. Cross-cultural cuisine with Mediterranean salads and a good version of *bryndzové halušky*. Housed in the

Powder Tower (*Prašná Bašta*), one of Bratislava's oldest buildings. Also try Café Kút connected in same courtyard. Daily lunch menu with soup and main (115Sk). Evening mains avg 300Sk. *Open daily 11.00–23.00.*

Tempus Fugit Sedlárska 5; ☏ 02 5441 4357; www.tempusfugit.sk [1 B2]
In a restored 15th-century Renaissance building (cellars date from as early as 12th century) right opposite the boorish Irish–Mexican stag destinations, Tempus Fugit adds a touch of class to Sedlárska. Intimate dining with an eclectic décor of grey pillars and minimalist seating, blending the old with the new. Speciality is whole roast suckling pig (3,000Sk or 5,900Sk for a minimum of four people). Mains 350–850Sk (avg 500Sk). *Open daily 10.00–01.00.*

Woch Františkánske námestie 7; ☏ 02 5443 2927; f 02 5443 2928; e info@woch.sk; www.woch.sk [1 C2]
Luxury restaurant with traditional old Pressburg dishes served within yellowing faux-medieval walls, packed with wrought iron and white linen. Named after a 13th-century knight who was the first burgher of the city and a lover of good food. The building was home to the last woman burned at the stake in Bratislava for being a witch (see box *Which Witch*, page 206). Live jazz music in the basement club section. Mains price 450–800Sk (avg 600Sk). *Restaurant open daily 11.00–midnight, club open daily 18.00–02.00.*

Zichy Café Restaurant Ventúrska 9; ☏ 02 5441 8557 [1 B3]
Elegant courtyard with a gargoyle spouting up out of the flagstones. A lot of pork dishes done in trendy styles (189Sk) and a tearoom underneath (Čajovňa open daily 14.00–23.00) if you want to check out Zichy's cellar. Mains 200Sk. *Open daily 10.00–23.00.*

Beyond the Old Town gates, Centrum and further afield

Alžbetka Mickiewiczova 1; ☏ 02 5292 3988; www.alzbetka.sk [3 F3]
Traditional restaurant in a nobleman's palace serves up Hungarian and Slovak portions. The venue was a favourite of local gourmets in the 1930s. Credit cards accepted. Mains 125–740Sk (avg 200Sk). *Open daily 11.00–23.00.*

Au Café Tyršovo nábrežie, Petržalka; ☏ 02 6252 0355; www.au-cafe.sk [4 E8]
Great setting on the Danube banks in the park. Au Café first opened in 1827. It offers Italian dishes in a very grey room and some of the yuppies are a little scary. Credit cards accepted. Mains 190–590Sk (avg 300Sk). *Open Sun–Thu 10.00–01.00, Fri–Sat 10.00–02.00.*

Bar Parada Hviezdoslavovo námestie 14; ☏ 0904 332 523 [1 C3]
Quiet, cavernous, Iberian-tinged bar and restaurant, refreshingly very light on the décor and theme-bar tat. Bare, yellowing walls, a dark and cool retreat from the beating sun. It feels like when you step outside you will be in Seville. Pasta, grilled meats, veggie meals and Czech lager, Pilsner Urquell (40Sk). A fat grilled trout (205Sk) and baked potato (40Sk) make a delicious dinner. Mains price 135–300Sk (avg 180Sk). *Open Mon–Thu 08.00–midnight, Fri 08.00–03.00, Sat 10.00–03.00, Sun 10.00–midnight.*

Caribic's Žižkova 1/A; ☏ 02 5441 8334; www.caribics.sk [4 A6]
Specialising in seafood. Popular, reliably good but pricey fish restaurant on the ground floor of a former fisherman's house down by the waterfront below the castle. Delicious stuffed squid on cherry tomatoes (489Sk), Caesar salad (299Sk), Krušovice imperial beer (55Sk). Credit cards accepted. Mains 299–699Sk (avg 489Sk). *Open daily 11.00–midnight (pension open 24/7).*

Chez David Zámocká 13; ☏ 02 5441 3824; www.chezdavid.sk [1 A2]
Kosher restaurant serving fresh, beautifully prepared Jewish cuisine. Closed on Saturdays. Also pension with seven dbl rooms, one sgl (See the *Accommodation* chapter). Credit cards accepted. Daily lunch menu 107Sk, soups 57Sk. Mains price 177–277Sk (avg 240Sk). *Open daily 11.30–22.00.*

Francúzska reštaurácia (Hotel Devín); Riečna 4; ☏ 02 5998 5852; www.hoteldevin.sk [1 B/C4]
Usually quite a deserted restaurant, which is a mystery because the food is excellent, but the staff often don't appear and potential diners wander off somewhere else. Don't let the brown furnishings put you off the delicious Gallic cuisine. Well-informed sommelier Štefan Valovič can advise on more than 200 Slovak wines. *Open daily 12.00–15.00 & 18.00–23.00.*

Gastro Hviezda Námestie 1 mája 15 [2 E3]
The 'Star' offers Slovak cuisine with pizza as the speciality in a canteen setting under garish lights. However, it is good for snacks after clubbing especially if you're staying at Hotel Tatra. The 'Weekend' (*vikendové*) menu costs 198Sk for soup, main course and dessert. *Open non-stop.*

Govinda Obchodná 30; ☏ 02 5296 2366; www.iskcon.sk [1 C1]
Run by the Slovak Hare Krishna community, the entirely vegetarian Govinda has some very tasty Indian meals for a good price. It's popular as a lunch and dinner venue, but also contains a small tea house and shop with oriental goods. *Open Mon–Fri 11.00–20.30, Sat 11.30–19.30, closed Sun.*

Happy Kebab (and Happy Pizza) Námestie SNP 7; \/f 02 5443 0383; e info@happy-kebab.sk; www.happy-kebab.sk [1 C2]
The best kebab shop in town, not greasy but stylish, with beautiful blue Turkish tiles. Offers all manner of snacks: kebabs (69Sk), soups (39Sk), salads (avg 60Sk), pizzas (120–170Sk) and grilled meats (140Sk). A great range of teas and coffees with Turkish tea (15Sk), Turkish coffee (25Sk). Try the divine vegetarian kebab (69Sk) or a big slab of pizza (40Sk) for a nourishing, filling and bargain lunch. *Open 11.00–midnight.*

Kozia Brana Kozia 21 entrance on Podjavorinskej ulica; \ 02 5443 0943 [1 A1]
Situated on a quiet back street, on the lower reaches of Slavin Hill, in an elegant turn-of-the-20th-century building. Kozia Brana is an old-style Czech restaurant recalling the pre-Velvet Revolution era. It is not a tourist venue so the menu may be tricky to decipher but the ambience is authentic small-town Czechoslovakia. Sturdy Czech cuisine with soups 29–34Sk, mains (a lot of grilled meat) 105–125Sk and a daily menu for 90Sk. Great choice of Czech beer. *Open Mon–Sat 09.00–23.00, Sun 11.00–22.00.*

Leberfinger Viedenská cesta 257; \ 02 6231 7590 [4 E8]
Traditional Pressburg specialities in a historic building visited by Napoleon. A great venue for an afternoon chow on the summer terrace. Situated near Au Café on the other side of the river. Mains 109–800Sk (avg 240Sk). *Open daily 11.00–midnight.*

Le Monde Hviezdoslavovo námestie 26; \ 0908 367 979, 0910 261 605; www.lemonde.sk [1 C3]
Bratislava's swankiest restaurant now in its newer, larger setting of the reconstructed Kern

House on Hviezdoslavovo námestie, Le Monde still offers great Mediterranean fare in a classy setting. *Open daily 11.00–midnight.*

Messina (Hotel Marrol's), Tobrucká 4; ℡ 02 5778 4600 [1 D4]
Named after the 15th-century Italian Renaissance painter Antonello da Messina, this arty restaurant is really classy. The wood-panelled, chandeliered Messina serves Italian food (figs, mascarpone, prosciutto, saffron, lamb, shrimps, 'fried chocolate lasagne!' – I dribble at the mere mention) and has already won scores of local awards. Mains price 190–895Sk (avg 500Sk). *Open Mon–Fri 06.30–10.00 & 11.30–23.00, Sat–Sun 07.00–10.00 & 11.30–23.00.*

Opera Brasserie (Radisson SAS Hotel Carlton), Hviezdoslavovo námestie 3; ℡ 02 5939 0400 [1 C4]
Swiss executive chef Markus Niederhauser lets his imagination run riot in the old-time setting. International cuisine, Slovak dishes done in a lighter fashion. Locally adapted international food. Veggie dishes (420Sk), soups (140–220Sk), salads (180–380Sk), tournedos Rossini, grilled lamb (680Sk), brochette de thon, gratin aux fruits de mer (520Sk), excellent patisserie for dessert, sorbets and crèmes glacées (60Sk), regional cheeses (250Sk). Mains price (480–680Sk). *Open Mon–Fri 06.30–22.30, Sat–Sun 07.00–10.30.*

People's Lounge Gorkeho 1; ℡ 02 5464 0777; www.peopleslounge.sk [1 C3]
Just across from the National Theatre, with boxy orange furniture and a cool Zen minimalism, this is a very NY chic diner. Tuna melt 171Sk, green salad 152Sk, grilled salmon 456Sk, beef medallions 589Sk, costly cocktails and languid clientele. Mains 171–589Sk (avg 600Sk). *Open Mon–Thu 10.00–01.00, Fri–Sat 10.00–02.00, Sun 10.00–01.00.*

Preego Zilinska 4; ☏ 0903 246 226; www.preego.sk [3 F1]
Hideous entrance up a fire escape-style stairway behind the inverted pyramid of Slovak
Radio cleverly conceals one of Bratislava's best-kept culinary secrets. If the stairs are like
something from South Central LA, the interior is pure uptown Manhattan. Classy lounge-
bar, with stylish lighting. The name is a strange pun and pronounced as three syllables pre
ego (For the ego) but also can be pronounced like the Italian prego (You're welcome).
Mains 250–400Sk (avg 300Sk). Credit cards accepted. *Café lounge open daily 10.00–midnight,
restaurant open daily 11.00–22.00.*

Savoyka Mostová 6 just behind the Carlton building; ☏ 02 5443 2002 [1 C4]
Ragout of mouflon with mashrooms (*sic*) and Vienna dumplings for 685Sk (€17.20) or eight
courses for 1,950Sk (€48.75) for a total blow-out. Located on the side of the Radisson SAS
Carlton Hotel building). *Open Mon–Fri 11.30–14.30, 18.30–23.30, Sat 18.00–23.00, Sun
closed.*

Slovenska Restauracia Hviezdoslavovo námestie 20; ☏ 02 5443 4883. www.slovrest.com
[1 C3]
Rustic restaurant with Hansel and Gretel furniture and cartwheels dangling from the walls,
and an (unintentionally) amusing menu. 'Selections of our old mothers' is not very flattering.
A good place to try Tokay. *Open daily 11.00–23.00.*

Sushi Bar Kikaku Gorkého 6; ☏ 02 5443 4783; www.kikaku.sk [1 D3]
Opened by a local lady who loves Japanese dishes and shows great swish with the fish.
Overpriced saki. Menu illustrated with photos for virgin sushi diners. Sirashu sushi and

Restaurants

sashimi mixes 540–560Sk, one piece Nigiri 60–80Sk. *Open May–Sep daily 11.30–23.00, Oct–Apr daily 11.30–22.00.*

Traja Musketieri Sládkovičova 7; ↘ 02 5443 0019; www.trajamusketieri.sk [2 D3]
The taste of 1625 is a creepy menu with recommendations from Athos and Porthos: 'I picked mushrooms in the morning dew thinking of you', 'Under the Corset' and even 'Silence of the Lambs'; might put you off your knightly splurge. Mains 145–495Sk (avg 295Sk). *Open 11.00–23.00.*

UFO Watch Taste Groove Nový most; ↘ 02 6252 0300; email:info@u-f-o.sk; www.u-f-o.sk [4 C8]
Difficult to place this venue as it's three things in one: Watch, Taste, Groove. Former Bystrica Café re-opened after two years' slumber to become the hippest, hottest venue in town. Sky-high café situated in the 'Lost in Space' flying saucer high above the city's main suspension bridge. Cover charge 150Sk. Membership from 5,000Sk. *Tickets for lift and Watch observation deck (open daily 10.00–22.00) 50Sk (€1.40). Taste (restaurant) open Sun–Fri 10.00–01.00, Sat 11.00–22.00. Groove (exclusive nightclub) open Sat 23.00–04.00.*

U Mamičky Palisády 40; ↘ 02 5441 1348; www.menu.sk/umamicky [2 C3]
Up in the hilly, residential part of town on walking route to the Slavin Monument, you'll find a classy Balkan place, owned by a Macedonian gentleman and featuring a gorgeous green garden. 'At Mummy's' features great Balkan food cooked to order on a charcoal grill with treats from the Adriatic every Tue & Thu. *Open Mon–Sun 11.00–23.00.*

U Zlatého Vodnika (At the Golden Waterman) Zlaté Piesky 15; ℡ 02 4425 9224
Ⓣ 2, 4, to Zlaté Piesky terminus
Massive portions in the little hut on the lake. Sit on the terrace overlooking the water and be sure to try the grilled trout with garlic. They do doggy bags too. Highly recommended. Mains avg 189Sk, Budweiser half-litre 29Sk, *čierne pivo* half-litre 39Sk. On the main road to Nitra and Žilina. *Open daily 09.00–23.00.*

Veža Restaurant Cesta na Kamzík 14; ℡ 02 4446 2774; www.restauraciaveza.sk
ⓉⒷ 203 from Hodžovo námestie to terminus, then 20 mins' walk uphill through woods
Built in 1975, the 200m tower reaches a height of 638m above sea level and gives a fantastic 360° panoramic view of Bratislava and all surrounding countryside as it rotates gently. Be careful where you put your handbag down as the outer and inner parts of the restaurant remain static and it may sail off. Slight seasickness may ensue in the sensitive. Décor is a creepy Habsburg/Soviet mélange. Mains 160–300Sk (avg 220Sk). *Open daily 11.00–midnight.*

CAFÉS AND TEAROOMS

Like its neighbours Vienna and Budapest, Bratislava has a long coffee-house tradition. Some traditional cafés still exist and many Slovaks love to while away an afternoon at the *cukráreň* (pâtisserie). On Sunday afternoons, they used to take the tram all the way to Vienna for a coffee, and the Viennese came to Pressburg (Bratislava) for their *kaffee und kuchen*.

Do the traditional thing and order a *viedenská káva* (a heart-blasting coffee topped with whipped cream) and strudel (*štrúdľa*) with poppyseed and curd cheese (*makovo-tvarohová*). Most places also serve cappuccinos, lattes and variations on the java jive. As in Vienna, you'll get a tiny biscuit or bit of chocolate and often a glass of water with your brew.

If you prefer tea, Bratislava has a growing collection of *čajovňa* or tearooms. Most are non-smoking and offer a variety of premium teas from all parts of the globe.

Other favourite cake items include *krémeš* (huge cubes of custard cream held in place with pastry), *bajgle* (glazed crescent-shaped rolls filled with walnuts or poppy seeds) and *šamrola* (pastries filled with cream and dusted with icing sugar).

Old Town and Castle District

Café Kút Zámočnícka 11; ☎ 02 5443 4957; www.kut.prasnabasta.sk [1 B/C2]
A cosy café hidden in a courtyard next to the Prašna Bašta restaurant, endless cocktail variations, cool tunes, DJs, reggae. *Open Mon–Fri 08.00–23.00, Sat–Sun 16.00–23.00.*

Čokoláda Michalská 6; ☎ 02 5443 3945 [1 B2]
The Austro-Hungarian nobility loved to go out for a hot choccie. Here they have 60 different kinds on offer including a weird concoction with tomato juice. *Open Mon–Fri 09.00–20.00, Sat–Sun 10.00–20.00.*

Kaffé Mayer Hlavné námestie 4 [1 C3]
An old-style Viennese kaffee und kuchen, one of three biggies on Hlavné námestie. Dark and reassuring with polished wood and great cakes. It even gets a mention in Patrick Leigh Fermor's *A Time of Gifts*. *Open Sun–Thu 09.30–22.00, Fri–Sat 09.30–midnight.*

Kaviareň Radnička Stará Radnička [1 C2/3]
One of the few non-smoking cafés in the city located under the arch leading to the City Museum in the Town Hall. Golden light twinkles on the wrought iron. *Open daily 09.30–21.00.*

London Café (British Council) Panská 17; ☎ 02 5443 1074 [1 C3]
Smart white café, with restaurant one side and café with two internet terminals the other. Large selection of daily papers and magazines from the UK. A great place to catch up on gossip and vitamins. *Open Mon–Fri 09.00–20.00, Sat 09.00–15.00, closed Sun.*

Malewill Café Uršulínska 9; ☎ 02 5443 4440 [1 C2]
Malewill has 20 versions of a cup of coffee. A Kava choco latte cost 46Sk. Strange and slightly sinister décor of a spider with daddy long legs made from tree branches and murals painted directly onto the ancient plaster. Delicious coffee, served in large white cups, little biccies. *Open Mon–Fri 10.00–midnight, Sat 12.00–midnight, Sun 12.00–22.00.*

Beyond the Old Town gates, Centrum and further afield
Bagel and Coffee Story Štúrova 13; ☎ 02 5263 1655; f 02 5263 1656; e bratislava@bagelcoffeestory.com; www.bratislava.bagelcoffeestory.com [1 E2]
The strangest (but strangely palatable) cup of tea (39Sk) ever, served in a huge cup with frothy cappuccino-style milk, but the Italian bagels (47Sk) are superb, fresh and filled with goodness. *Open Mon–Fri 07.30–22.00, Sat 08.30–22.00, Sun 10.00–21.00.*

Cafés and tea rooms

Café Múzeum Vajanského nábrežie 2; ↘ 07 5296 5681 [1 D4]

Delightful place at the back of the Natural History Museum or you can get in around the back. Cavernous hall, echoing marble steps leading up at each side. Good selection of snacks, drinks (beer and hot chocolate). Very peaceful, people eating salads for lunch, meeting a secret lover for a tryst, hushed tones. *Open daily 09.00–21.00.*

Café Propeler Rázusovo nábrežie 1; ↘ 02 5400 1020 [4 E7]

Alfresco dining overlooking the grey-green Danube is tempting on a warm summer's evening. Grilled meats and fish followed by ice cream make tasty suppers. There's also a Propeler Grill over the river in Sad Janka Kráľa (park) open in summer and offering grilled meats and sausages. Mains avg 107Sk. *Open Tue–Sun 10.00–23.00.*

Domenico Námestie Ľ. Štúra 4; ↘ 02 5464 0167 [1 C4]

Situated in the Esterházy Palace, this roomy old venue was previously the Berlinka and recalls the old Viennese coffee-house tradition. Popular with the granny-hat-and-cake brigade. Lots of OAPs seem to be on the sauce. Daily lunch menu 99Sk, mains avg 170Sk. *Open daily 10.00–22.00.*

Veža Café Cesta na Kamzík 14; ↘ 02 4446 2774; www.restauraciaveza.sk

TB *203 from Hodžovo námestie to terminus, then 20 mins' walk uphill through woods*

Situated on the floor above the restaurant, the bar doesn't spin round, which perhaps is just as well as the clanking lift is enough to make you dizzy with nerves. The lift sounds like a wind tunnel and the café shakes in the breeze; you'll need a swift half (330ml of Budvar for 38Sk) to calm your nerves. The café throbs slightly and feels like it's alive. There's another café on the ground floor for vertigo sufferers or those easily offended by the hideous 1970s theme park Maria Theresa-style décor. *Open daily 11.00–02.00.*

BARS, PUBS AND CLUBS
Old Town and Castle District

De Zwaan Panská 7; ℡ 02 5441 9166; www.dezwaan.sk [1 C3]
Belgian-owned pub with Leffe beer on tap, De Zwaan recalls an Amsterdam brown café: cosy, dark, restful, very laid-back Low Countries. Selection of Flemish and Walloon cuisine. Non-smoking area makes a refreshing change in a ciggie-loving city. *Open daily 11.00–23.00.*

Dubliner Irish Pub Sedlárska 6; ℡ 02 5441 0706; www.irish-pub.sk [1 B3]
Getting a bit grubby and whiffy around the edges these days, but a comforting venue where you don't have to dress up to drink Guinness. Packed with expats, stag parties and bewildered-looking locals. *Open Mon–Sat 11.00–03.00, Sun 11.00–01.00.*

Kristián Pub Michalská 10; ℡ 02 5443 4038 [1 B2]
Don't be deterred by the very oniony aroma as you descend the stairs to the cellar bar. The stair walls have grapes and vines painted onto very yellow walls; the bright green and yellow is very cheerful and sets the tone. Fabulous beer, the best-kept draught Pilsner in Bratislava, perhaps in Slovakia, says the barman proudly (39Sk for half-litre of Pilsner Urquell – chilled and delicious). See *Internet cafés,* pages 97–8. *Open daily 14.00–midnight.*

Verdict Bar Panská 6; ℡ 0910 930 143 [1 C3]
The jury's still out on this one; it's quite nondescript, but a pleasant enough place to sip a

cold beer and watch the footie, if the ice hockey isn't on. As with everywhere in Bratislava, cocktails rule the bar show. International bar food. *Open Mon–Thu 11.00–midnight, Fri–Sat 11.00–01.00, Sun 14.00–midnight.*

Vináreň Velké Františkáni Františkánske námestie 10; ☏ 02 5443 3073 [1 C2] The most famous wine cellar in town, in a late Renaissance building dating from 1347. A selection of 130 Slovak wines on offer within the bricked-up vaults. Live Gypsy music every night from 18.00. A lively and entertaining evening out (see also Malí Františkáni at Námestie SNP 24 in the following section). When you totter out look up at the bedroom window from where a Franciscan monk gesticulates gleefully. Mains avg 200Sk. *Restaurant open daily 11.00–01.00, wine cellar open daily 17.00–01.00.*

Beyond the Old Town gates, Centrum and further afield

Bistro Čajka Nábrežie arm.gen. Ľ. Svobodu (next to Botel Marína) [4 A7] A delightful little stone hut, its walls painted with seagulls (*čajka*) flying across a sky blue sky. In late spring, out come three tables by the gangplank down to the Botel Marína and a lucky few can sit and sip a cool beer by the Danube, in the shade of tall trees. Offers Stein beer, founded in 1873 in Bratislava, then called *Prešporok*. *Open daily 16.00–22.00.*

Gremium Gorkého 10; ☏ 02 5413 1025; f 02 5443 0653; e cherrytour@mail.pvt.sk; www.gremium.sk [1 D3] Busy sports bar, with a big screen and banks of TVs dangling from the ceiling showing ice hockey and football. Ticket office with betting (a bit like the pools) on sports matches.

Guinness (80Sk), bagels (29–45Sk) and jumbo coffees (49Sk). Unusually, amongst the young, hip bar staff, nobody speaks English. *Open daily 11.00–midnight.*

KGB Obchodná 52; ☎ 02 5273 1278 [1 C1]
A rather claustrophobic cellar pub that may drive you to drink. Fortunately there's a range of *pivo* and *pivo*-absorbing dishes. Clichéd commie theme has Lenin, Stalin and Gustáv Husák, Czechoslovakia's last communist leader, although the name is an abbreviation for Krčma Gurmánov Bratislavy (Pub of Bratislava Gourmets). *Open Mon–Thu 11.00–01.30, Fri 11.00–03.30, Sat 15.30–01.00, Sun 15.30–23.00.*

Korzo Hviezdoslavovo námestie 11; ☎ 02 5443 4974 [1 B4]
Windy terrace with tourist prices but a great place to sip Zlatý Bažant (50Sk), soak up the sun and stare at the cars whizzing over Nový most. Home-made puddings, a selection of daily papers and a restaurant downstairs featuring live folk music. Something on the menu called 'fried bull's glads'. *Open daily 08.00–midnight.*

Malí Františkáni (Little Franciscans) Námestie SNP 24; ☎ 02 5413 1236 [1 C2]
For those who want to continue drinking until late, finding this cellar bar is just the start of the task. Then you have to negotiate a labyrinth of low-ceilinged corridors leading to a medieval room with some monk memorabilia. A cool venue on hot days. *Open daily 10.00–06.00.*

Sparx Cintorínska 32; ☎ 02 5296 8061, 0903 403 097; e rezervacie@sparx.sk; www.sparx.sk [3 H4]
Formerly the Mamut (Mammoth) Pub (www.mamut.sk), once the largest beer hall in central Europe packing in 2,000 drinkers, now this vast complex includes a pub, cocktail bar, restaurant,

disco, nightclub, strip joint, bingo hall, casino, internet café and self-service lunch canteen. The cavernous Stará sladovňa was built in 1872 next to the Stein brewery and was the city's malthouse until 1976. The spirit of the beer hall lives on around the corner on Ferienčikova 3 at Mamutík, a kind of Mini-Mamut. 'This town ain't big enough for the both of us' could be the theme tune but that's about as far as the link with Ron and Russell Mael's pop group goes. *Open Mon–Wed 10.00–midnight, Thu–Fri 10.00–03.00, Sat 11.00–03.00, Sun 11.00–midnight.*

Trafená Hus Šafárikovo námestie 7; ☎ 02 5292 5473; www.trafenahus.sk [1 E4]
The name comes from the saying *Trafená hus zagága* (literally: the struck goose squeals) meaning a person with a guilty conscience who unwillingly lets the cat out of the bag. The terrible smell as you enter doesn't seem to put anyone else off as by 17.00 on a Friday evening all the tables have a 'reserved' sign. Tall rickety stools line up against the long tall bar; dangerously high after several cocktails. A lot of Belgian beer. *Open Mon–Fri 07.00–midnight, Sat–Sun 10.00–midnight.*

Umelka Dostojevského 2; ☎ 02 5263 4754; www.umelka.sk [1 E4]
A '*pivný* pub' (or 'beer pub'; what other kinds are there?) opposite Komenského University; shady terrace spoilt by exhaust fumes from Old Bridge traffic. It's famous as the venue for a photo of man challenging a Soviet tank in 1968. Inside is a fairly basic, honest-to-goodness Slovak pub, woody interior designed by organic woodcarver Peter Strassner. Grumpy barman, and alcohol in every shape and form. *Open Mon–Fri 10.00–23.00, Sat–Sun 11.00–23.00.*

Verne Hviezdoslavovo námestie 18; ☎ 02 5443 0514 [1 C3]
Arty students crowd this venue done up with decorations based on Jules Verne's stories. 'It's

like sitting in somebody's living room,' notes a Danish visitor. A charming café with antique furniture and unique decorations based on the novels by Jules Verne. Popular with lunch menu crowd. Outdoor seating in summer. *Open Mon–Thu 08.30–midnight, Fri 08.30–01.00, Sat 10.00–01.00, Sun 11.00–midnight.*

Bistro Zora Karadzicova 47; ☎ 55 410 791/ 815 429 [3 J1]
Situated a little out of the centre, but a good destination to see real Slovak entertainment, Zora is 'your generation pub'. A smoky beer hall which, on Saturday lunchtime, has live music with a band fronted by a middle-aged woman singing '70s and old-time hits as well as Slovak pop. *Open Mon–Fri 09.00–22.00, Sat 10.00–22.00, Sun 14.00–22.00.*

1 Slovenská krčma/1st Slovak Pub Obchodná 62; ☎/f 02 5292 6367; e
slovakpub@slovakpub.sk; www.slovakpub.sk [1 C1]
Pink building on dusty Obchodná, this pub is made up of 11 separate rooms, some spacious, some cramped representing various periods in Slovakia's history – such as Janosik's Room, dedicated to the prince of thieves. Cottage done up like a *chata* from the Líptov region, and an unlikely place to sup a beer, the Room of St Cyril and St Method, the creators of the written Slav language. 'Grandmother's favourite' dishes to accompany the wide selection of drinks. *Open Mon–Thu 10.00–midnight, Fri–Sat 10.00–02.00, Sun 12.00–midnight.*

17s Bar Hviezdoslavovo námestie 17; ☎ 02 5443 5135; www.17bar.sk [1 C3]
Great pizza served until late and Czech beer on draught. Seating in cosy alcoves. Live music. *Open daily 12.00–midnight.*

7 Entertainment, nightlife and recreation

In the spring and summer and even early autumn, Bratislava's Old Town comes alive in the late afternoon as the pavement cafés fill with people enjoying an aperitif or chilled beer in the sunshine before heading off to a restaurant, show or another bar.

The pretty, tree-lined Hviezdoslavovo námestie is crowded with people dressed up in their glad rags, gathering before a performance at the Slovak National Theatre or the Reduta. Even if your mission is to drink Bratislava dry, you should consider a night at the opera. You will never again have such a great opportunity to see world-class singers in a gorgeous setting for the price of a pint in London.

Pick up a copy of *Kam do Mesta*, the pocket-sized monthly listings guide or check out the entertainments pages of the *Slovak Spectator*.

TICKET OFFICES
Slovak National Theatre (opera) tickets SND Ticket Office, Komenského námestie (behind the SND building). Tickets may be purchased starting three months in advance: Mon–Fri 08.00–17.30, Sat 09.00–13.00; \f 02 5443 3764. Standby tickets at the ticket office in the SND's Historical Building foyer 30 minutes before the performances. There are two prices as tickets go on sale three months before performances. In the unlikely event that there are still some tickets left, they can be purchased up to ten days before the show for

as little as €2 in the second balcony. As a guide to prices, tickets cost €15–30 (last-minute unsold tickets from €3.50) for *Turandot*, €10–25 for *Aida* (last-minutes from €3). For some lesser-known operas, eg: *The Kiss*, regular tickets cost €2.50–10.

Slovak Philharmonic Slovensky filharmónie, Reduta building; Palackého 2. Reservations ☏ 02 5920 8233 or 02 5920 8211; f 02 5443 5956; e filharmonia@filharmonia.sk; www.filharmonia.sk. *Ticket office open Mon, Tue, Thu, Fri 13.00–19.00, Wed 08.00–14.00 and one hour before performances.*

BKIS Klobučnícka 2 sells tickets; ☏ 02 5443 2708

Eventim Tickets online at www.eventim.sk

Ticket Portal offices can be found in the shopping malls Aupark, Polus City Center and in the tourist offices of Satur and Hydrotour. Tickets online at www.ticketportal.sk; ☏ 02 5293 3323.

THEATRE

Bratislava has a strong theatrical tradition, and while most performances will be in Slovak and out of reach for many visitors' ears, the Slovak National Theatre is a must for opera or ballet and venues such as the Puppet Theatre and the more alternative Stoka may have shows that appeal. Musicals, showing at the Nová scéna and sometimes at the beautiful Aréna, go down well in any language.

Slovak National Theatre (Opera and Ballet) Hviezdoslavovo námestie 1; ☏ 02 5443 3083; www.snd.sk. The beautifully restored Slovak National Theatre dates back to 1776 and offers drama, ballet and opera. *Aida, Turandot, The Merry Widow, Tosca, Eugene Onegin* and *Peter Grimes* are the big draws of the 2006 season. *Summer break Jul–Aug. Season runs Sep–Jun.*

Aréna Viedenská cesta 10; ☏ 02 6720 2553. Situated in Sad Janka Kráľa (park) next to the Old Bridge. The oldest theatre in Bratislava, built in 1828 and showing daring and controversial plays, such as the recent *Tiso*; the director is the highly esteemed actor Juraj Kukura.

Astorka Korzo '90 (Playhouse) Suché mýto 17; ☏ 02 5443 1657. A small drama group giving well-regarded dramatic performances. *Shows at 19.30.*

Malá scena Dostojevského rad 7; ☏ 02 5292 3773

Nová scéna SND Kollárovo námestie 20; ☏ 02 5292 5741. A venue for musicals, and very popular in the last decade. *Shows at 19.00.*

Puppet Theatre Dunajska 36; ☏ 02/ 529 23 668; e bbdbrtis@stonline.sk; www.babkovedivadlo.sk. Performances for children and adults with a rich and varied repertoire. *Performances usually at 10.00 and 14.00.*

Stoka Pribinova 1; ☏ 02 5292 4463

Studio L+S Námestie 1 mája 5; ☏ 02 5292 1130

Theatre of P O Hviezdoslav Laurinská 21; ☏ 02 5443 3083

MUSIC
Classical music

Given Bratislava's rich musical heritage – visitors have included such luminaries as Liszt, Mozart, Beethoven, Bartók, Dohnanyi, Haydn as well as local boy Hummel – you'd be mad to miss a classical music production while in the presence of such greats.

The buildings of the Slovak National Theatre and the Reduta are beautiful historic monuments and the opera productions rival those in Budapest and Vienna for a much more reasonable price. Those who can only dream of attending a performance at Covent Garden or New York's Met can take in several shows of comparable quality and enjoyment in Bratislava and still have change left to buy dinner afterwards.

Visit the elegant Mirbach and the Primate's Palace to hear chamber music concerts or piano recitals in an atmospheric setting. You can also catch many excellent choirs for free if you pop into churches such as the Lutheran church in the Old Town. The bizarre inverted pyramid building of the Slovak radio has amazing acoustics.

Bratislava Castle Concert Hall ☎ 02 5441 4300
Slovak Philharmonic, Reduta Palackého 2; ☎ 02 5443 3351; www.filharm.sk. On the same square is the Reduta concert hall, home of the Slovak Philharmonic, one of the best orchestras in central Europe. Daily classical concerts cost from £5.
Moyzes' Concert Hall Vajanského nábrežie 12; ☎ 02 5443 3351
Klarisky Concert Hall Farská 4, Church of the Sisters of the Order of St Clare; ☎ 02 5443 2942; www.mksba.sk
Mirbach Palace Františkánske námestie 11; ☎ 02 5443 1556. *Concerts every Sunday at 11.30.*
Mirror Hall of the Primate's Palace Primaciálne námestie; ☎ 02 5935 6111
Music Centre Slovakia Michalská 10; ☎ 02 5443 4003; www.hc.sk. Has a list of events: jazz, blues, classical.
Slovak Radio Concert Hall (Slovenský roshlas) Mýtna 1; ☎ 02 5727 3479

Music

MUSICAL HERITAGE

Franz Liszt Ventúrska 7 in Leopold di Pauli Palace (next to Zichy Palace). In 1820 Liszt (1811–86) aged nine gave a concert in the garden pavilion and started on his triumphal career. Also a bust of Liszt on Rudnayavo námestie.

Béla Bartók Klariská ulica. Hungarian Bartók (1881–1945) studied Slovak folk songs here 1892–99. Bust of Bartók in pink stone, head emerging from stone at Spitalska 7. He lived and worked here 1894–1908 – near the Sv Ladislav church; monastery at number 5.

Ernő Dohnányi (1877–1960) Hungarian composer/pianist studied at the Catholic School at the Convent of Clare Nuns on Klariská ulica.

Wolfgang Amadeus Mozart (1756–91) Ventúrska 10, Pálffy Palace. Mozart aged six gave a concert (accompanied by his father) for local aristocracy in 1762; also his *Requiem* was performed in St Martin's Cathedral in 1834.

Ludwig van Beethoven Panska ulica 27. Beethoven gave a concert at Earl Keglevich's Baroque palace here.

Johann Nepomuk Hummel Klobučnícka 2. Hummel was born here, now a museum to his life and work.

Joseph Haydn Kapitulská. Haydn conducted the premiere of his opera *La Canterina* here at the former Esterházy Palace, Kapitulská 6.

Concert halls

Bratislava has some massive halls and attracts a mix of international bands and world stars and the more modest local singers. Musicals and big spectaculars are also popular. You will also find a Twilight Zone aspect to live music in Bratislava. Bands and singers you thought had long since given up touring for a life of slippers and cutting the lawn are still playing here, some more welcome memories than others. Demis Roussos and Janis Joplin's original backing band, Big Brother and the Holding Company have helped to give the city a sleepy, lotus-eaters ambience, a little stranded in the 1970s at times.

Babylon Music Club Karpatska 2; ☎ 02 5249 8005. Formerly a cinema, this boxy-shaped music hall with loads of neon hosts domestic and regional music acts almost daily. Ghymes (who are known for performing Slovak folk music in Hungary) play here frequently.

Incheba www.incheba.sk. Seal performed recently at one of the many huge pavilions.

Istropolis Trnavské mýto 1; ☎ 02 5557 4939. Recent spectaculars at this cavernous venue include the *Galileo* musical and a performance by Stomp!

PKO Nábrežie arm gen Ľ. Svobodu 3; ☎ 02 5441 6040. BKIS puts on concerts here like Omara Portuondo, country music festival.

Š H Pasienky Trnavská cesta 29; ☎ 02 4437 2127. Huge stadium home to Inter Slovnaft Bratislava basketball team. Concerts by Demis Roussos and the like.

ST Arena near Polus Center. Ice hockey arena used for spectaculars such as *Holiday on Ice*.

Music

Folk music

Many restaurants in Bratislava have folk music performances to accompany the food. Downstairs at the Korzo restaurant is particularly good. Large folk music performances can be seen at venues such as Istropolis. Bratislava's districts are dotted with culture houses where you can see performances or take part in a '**dance house**' (tanečný dom), a combination of folk dance lesson and performance. www.tanecnydom.sk explains more and has details of upcoming events.

Sluk Balkanska 31, Rusovce; ☎ 02 6285 9125. A folk ensemble, performs Slovak music and dance in and around Bratislava. Folk traditions from all over Slovakia are represented in unique arrangements.

Jazz and easy listening

Bratislavans are mad about jazz and there are many places to hear live concerts in a funky setting, often with food and drink to accompany the cool tunes. The International Jazz Festival is one of the most popular events of its kind in central Europe. It takes place at the PKO cultural centre on the banks of the Danube.

Nu Spirit Bar Medená 16; www.nuspirit.sk. Formerly Buddha Bar, Nu Spirit has a new look but same easygoing attitude. Features top DJs playing cool tunes. *Open Mon–Fri 12.00–02.00, Sat–Sun 15.00–midnight.*

Café Studio Club Laurinská 13. A good place for live jazz music, with artists such as the local favourite saxophonist Peter Cardarelli.

Jazz Café Ventúrska 5; ☏ 02 5443 4661. Cellar bar with live music, not just jazz, serving food too. Packed on Saturdays when there's usually Irish music. *Open daily 10.00–02.00.*
Metro Club Suché mýto 6. Near the Crowne Plaza Hotel, plays jazz and nostalgic grooves until late. *Open Fri–Sat 20.00–04.00.*
Radosť Obchodná 48; www.mojaradost.sk. A new chill-out bar attracting a hip young crowd. *Open Mon–Sat 17.00–04.30, Sun 17.30–midnight.*

Contemporary

Live rock music is still very popular and reggae goes down well too. Check out www.reggae.sk for more details.

Alligator Laurinská 7. Blues and rock from rough 'n' ready young bands.
Nultý Priestor Námestie SNP 12. The name means Zero Space, also connected to A4 club (www.a4.sk) providing a venue for non-commercial groups and individuals to put on shows of theatre, dance, music, cinema and any form of creative art. Workshops and discussion groups also held here. 'Plug-in Café' www.multispace.sk.
Stoka Pribinova 1; ☏ 02 5292 4470. This alternative theatre offers live blues, world music and grunge/rock concerts three times a week. Discussions by independent, alternative groups, concerts and other theatrical shows. *Performances usually at 20.00.*

NIGHTCLUBS AND DISCOS

When the lights go down, Bratislava becomes party central. There are many places where the beautiful people go to swing their pants.

Cirkus Barok Rázusovo nábrezie; ☏ 02/ 5464 2091–3; www.cirkusbarok.sk. Disco boat a couple of strokes upsteam from Botel Gracia near Námestie Ľ. Štúra. Daily lunch menu for 96Sk and in the evenings, themes such as the Mexican erotic night, 'I love disco' and 'After Work Party 3'. *Open daily 14.00–06.00.*

Duna Radlinského 11; www.duna.sk. Another bar in a bunker. This industrial club has rock, heavy metal and live DJs and is popular with a young underground crowd.

Elam VŠ Klub Staré grunty 53; ☏ 02 6542 6304; www.elam.sk. *Open Mon–Fri 16.00–01.00, Sat 16.00–04.30, Sun 16.00–01.00.*

Flamenko Music Club 14 Štefánikova; m 0905 612 904. Dance until 05.00 on weekends to spirited Latino music with laid-back patrons interested in having fun. *Open Mon–Thu 11.00–02.00, Fri 11.00–05.00, Sat 14.00–05.00, closed Sun.*

Harley Davidson Rebarbarova 1/a, Ružinov; ☏ 02 4319 1095. A ten-minute taxi ride away from the centre near the Slovnaft refinery – if you fancy strippers, grungy bikers and rock 'n' roll. *Open Mon–Fri 11.00–02.00, Sat–Sun 11.00–06.00.*

Hystéria Pub Odbojárov 9; ☏ 02 4445 4495. A young crowd chills here with two underground floors of varied electronica. *Open Fri–Sat 21.00–04.00.*

Krater Club Vysoka 14. Weekend live concerts alternate with disco nights and strip shows in this split-level nightspot. *Gay nights on Sat.*

Laverna 1224 Namestie SNP 24; ☏ 02 5443 3165; www.laverna.sk. A cellar disco with two bars, quieter table seating and a DJ-backed dance floor. A favourite with celebrities and the in-crowd. *Oldies disco every Tue. Open daily until 06.00.*

Spojka Prešernova 4; ☏ 0905 504 152; www.spojka.com. Groovy club near the Danube

STAG PARTIES – VOCABULARY

Slovak women are famous for their high-cheekboned beauty; with the cheap beer and beautiful women, thoughts of those on a stag trip to Bratislava will immediately turn to romance – tread carefully if you're the groom-to-be.

What's your name?	*Ako sa voláte?*
Can I buy you a drink?	*Môžem Vás pozvať na pohárik?*
Two beers, please	*Dvakrát pivo, prosím*
Cheers!	*Na zdravie!*
You drink like a fish (literally like a rainbow)	*Piješ ako dúha*
Where do you live?	*Kde bývate?*
What's your phone number?	*Aké máte telefónne číslo?*
Let's go to the cinema!	*Poďme do kina!*
May I have this dance?	*Môžem si s Vami zatancovať?*
You are the most charming lady (I have ever met)	*Si najpôvabnejšia mlada žena (s akou som sa kedy stretol)*
Are you married? (to a female/male)	*Ste vydatá/ženatý?*
I love you	*Ľúbim ťa*
I really love you (literally I love you like a horse)	*Ľúbim ťa ako koňa*

Nightclubs and discos

offering techno, R 'n' B, jazz and Afrobeat. Tickets online at www.eventim.sk or at the door. Just behind the Slovak National Museum.

Subclub Nábrézie arm. gen. Ľ. Svobodu; m 0904 949105; www.subclub.sk. A former nuclear fall-out shelter provides a slightly weird setting for drum 'n' bass, jungle, hiphop, techno.

Unique VŠ Club Staré grunty 36; m 0905 435 661; www.uniqueclub.sk. For a younger, studenty crowd, Unique at the university dormitories has jazz, soul and disco nights.

Strip clubs

It's best to ask your friendly concierge at the hotel or your stag party hostess about the hottest events at the time, as what they show and who they cater for may vary from night to night. Many venues such as Bellevue, Big Apple, Harley Davidson, Jalta Bar, Kráter Pub and Labyrint Club have different events each night.

Laverna 1224 Námestie SNP 11. *Different shows midweek. Wed – women, Thu – men.*
Moulin Rouge Casino Cintorínska 32. The best strip club in town.
Paradise Seberíniho 9; ☎ 02 4341 1592; f 02 4333 6420; e hotel@hotelbratislava.sk; www.hotelbratislava.sk. Topless dancers, table striptease and 'lesbi show'. *Shows 21.00–04.00.*
Smirnoff Safarikovo námestie 7; ☎ 02 5292 5472; e smirnoff@smirnoffclub.sk; www.smirnoffclub.host.sk. *Strip shows on Fri.*

Casinos

Bratislava has five top casinos with all the tables you'd expect and certain rules regarding minimum/maximum bet, currencies allowed. Check with the concierge.

Casino Café Reduta Medena 3; ☎ 02 5443 2021, 02 5443 2033; 📠 02 5443 1006; www.casinos.sk. The casino offers American and French roulette, blackjack, oasis poker with progressive super bonus, as well as a casino bar and restaurant. The entrance is free and punters can now play in euros. *Open daily 13.00–04.00.*

Demar Klub Kasino Pri šajbach 12, Rača; ☎ 02 4488 0477; www.demarklub.sk. A taxi-ride away in Rača, Demar has roulette and blackjack plus a restaurant, pool tables and bowling. *Open Mon–Thu 10.00–02.00, Fri 10.00–04.00, Sat 11.00–04.00, Sun 11.00–02.00.*

Moulin Rouge Casino Cintorínska ulica. Casino with two jackpots, neon flashing prize money totals. Rather tasteless as it is just in front of the main cemetery entrance.

Park Casino Hviezdoslavovo námestie 21; ☎ 02 5443 1669. No slot machines but seven gaming tables including roulette, blackjack and one poker table. *Open daily 13.00–05.00.*

Regency Casino Crowne Plaza Hotel, Hodžovo námestie 2; ☎ 02 5443 2377. Roulette from €1, blackjack from €2; punto banco and poker. The casino features 17 gaming tables: 8 American roulette, 7 blackjack, 2 Caribbean stud poker. Three restaurants. *Open daily 13.00–05.00.*

Senator Roulette Rybarska brána opposite Mezzo Mezzo restaurant. More of a bar, with some fruit machines, four electronic roulette machines and showing live sports on television. *Open daily 09.00–06.00.*

Gay Bratislava

The gay scene in Bratislava is quiet and discreet and there are few options for a big night out for gay men, even fewer for lesbians. Try putting out a few feelers in the Antik café if your gaydar senses the right person to ask. Drag shows are called 'travestie' nights – say no more. Check out www.gay.sk, www.gayinfo.sk or www.gayguide.net.

Apollon Panenská 24; www.apollon-gay-club.sk. Bratislava's coolest gay club is tucked into a vaulted cellar with two bars and a friendly atmosphere. Their website has many useful links. Strippers on Wed. *Open daily 18.00–02.00.*

Café Antik Rybanska brána 2. Has a mixed, gay-friendly crowd.

Caffé Barbaros Vysoká 20; ✆ 0903 461 717; www.barbaros.sk. This café opened May 2004 and soon became one of the most popular gay meeting places. *Lesbian day every Thu. Open Mon–Thu 09.00–01.00, Fri 09.00–03.00, Sat 17.00–03.00, Sun 18.00–midnight.*

Kráter Club Vysoká 42; www.kraterclub.sk. *Gay party on Sat nights.*

Spider Jedlíkova 9. *Open Sun–Thu 17.00–02.00, Fri–Sat 17.00–05.00.*

CINEMA

You can catch all the latest Hollywood blockbusters at gigantic multiplexes. Many are in the original language with subtitles in Slovak and/or Czech. Comedies and children's movies are usually dubbed. If you want to see a film look out for ST (with Slovak subtitles), ČT (with Czech subtitles) and be wary of films with SD (Slovak dubbing) or ČD (Czech dubbing). ČV means it's the Czech version. When looking for a film make sure it is *na tento týždeň* meaning 'showing this week'.

Palace Aupark (Multiplex) Einsteinova 18; ✆ 02/ 6820 2222; e aupark@palacecinemas.sk; www.palacecinemas.sk

CINEMATIC SETTINGS

Recently, while forced to watch *The Peacemaker* (1997), in which George Clooney saves New York from a nuclear explosion and some stereotypical Serb nationalists, I suddenly thought the car chase scene looked familiar. Gorgeous George and Nicole Kidman were smashing up cars belonging to sinister east European thugs right in the middle of Hviezdoslavovo námestie.

Recently, the cavernous cellars at Červeny Kameň Castle had some of its interior décor rearranged for a British film about Frankenstein.

Slovakia's stunning scenery, the high-quality Koliba and L+S studios and the favourable economic climate make the country a top destination for film companies. You can spot bits of Blava in *Behind Enemy Lines* (2001) with Gene Hackman and Owen Wilson, *The Living Daylights* (1987) with Timothy Dalton as 007, *Dragonheart* (1996) with Dennis Quaid, *Blue Moon* (2002), *Liszt's Rhapsody* (1996) and the UK serialisation of *Doctor Zhivago* (2002) starring Keira Knightley and Sam Neill.

Ster Century Multikino Metropolis Vajnorská 100, Polus City Center; ☏ 02 4910 2222; e info@multikinometropolis.sk; www.multikinometropolis.sk
Orange IMAX Avion Shopping Park, Ivánska cesta 12; ☏ 02 4342 3033; e info@kinoimax.sk; www.kinoimax.sk

Cinema

Hviezda Námestie 1 mája; ℡ 02 5296 7471
Mladosť Hviezdoslavovo námestie 14; ℡ 02 5443 5003
Tatra Námestie 1 mája, 12; ℡ 02/ 592 72 151
Filmový Klub Ic.sk Špitálska 4; ℡ 02/ 5296 3396
Filmový Klub Múzeum Old Town Hall; ℡ 02 5443 4742
Filmový Klub Nostalgia Starohorská 2; ℡ 02 5296 1712; www.nostalgia.sk

SPORTS
Passive sports
Bars in Bratislava show a lot of sports, particular during the colder months when guests sit indoors instead of sunning themselves on the pavement terrace. Ice hockey is extremely popular and a Slovan Bratislava match will take priority over Real Madrid, Bayern Munich, AC Milan or Chelsea football matches.

Dubliner Irish Pub Sedlárska 6; ℡ 02 5441 0706; www.irish-pub.sk [1 B3, 4 D5]. Shows ice hockey, football and some American sports. *Open Mon–Sat 11.00–03.00, Sun 11.00–01.00.*
Football Pub Pri Starom Háji; ℡ 02 6280 4428. Behind ArtMedia Bratislava football ground in Sad Janka Kráľa (park). Peppermint-coloured one-storey building with huge terrace with wooden benches. Pilsner Urquell, Budvar, Velvet, Staropramen. *Open Sun–Thu 11.00–midnight, Fri–Sat 11.00–01.00.*
Gremium Gorkého 10; ℡ 02 5413 1025; www.gremium.sk [1 D3, 4 E5]. (A huge screen at one end of the bar and banks of TVs above eye-level.) *Open daily 11.00–midnight.*

Mlyn Restaurant 18 Stará Prievozska, Mlynské Nivy; ☏ 02 5341 9948 [3 K4]. A little out of the centre towards the bus station, this rustic restaurant features Saturday rock concerts and big-screen sports.

Verdict Bar Panská 6; ☏ 0910 930 143 [1 C3, 4 D6]. TV showing ice hockey and Champions League football.

Bowling alleys

Brunswick Bowling Aupark Mall, Einsteinova 18; ☏ 02 6826 6456. *Open Mon–Thu 12.00–midnight, Fri–Sat 11.00–02.00, Sun 11.00–midnight.*

Chameleon Bowling Club Polus City Center, Vajorská 100; ☏ 02 4444 1133. Six lanes, booking essential. *Open daily 13.00–01.00.*

Kolkáreň Pasienky Trnavská 29/a; ☏ 02 4437 2101. Bowling hall with six lanes. Pub attached. *Open daily 10.00–22.00.*

Climbing

Indoor wall Boulderoom situated in the Petržalka district at Farského 24; ☏ 0905 787 193; e info@boulderoom.sk; www.boulderoom.sk. 🅱 78, 83, 84, 88, 92, 95, 99. Has a wide variety of indoor climbing possibilities. A two-hour ticket costs 80Sk for adults, 70Sk for students, 40Sk for children. Shoes, towels and hairdryers for hire, training courses offered, snacks and drinks available. *Open daily 10.00–22.00.*

Climbers also practise their skills on the wall of the Jewish cemetery at Žižkova, near Sorea Hotel.

Sports

Canoeing
Down the Danube to Čunovo and Gabčikovo is extremely popular.

Cycling
Very popular; many bike routes. For cycle tours see *Chapter 3*, page 102, and for cycle routes see *Chapter 11*, page 228.

Fitness centres
Most of the four-star hotels have their own fitness centres, open to the general public for a fee.

Golem Club (fitness centre) Aupark, Einsteinova 18; ℘ 02 6353 0891. *Open Mon–Fri 07.00–22.00, Sat–Sun 09.00–22.00.*

Zora Centrum Vajnorská 98; ℘ 02 4446 2404; e zoracentrum@zoracentrum.sk; www.zoracentrum.sk. Range of fitness programmes such as aerobics, fit-ball, fat-burner, kick-boxing, cardio workouts, step. *Open Mon–Fri 08.00–22.00, Sat–Sun 09.00–21.00.*

Football – teams
Bratislava boasts three teams: Slovan Bratislava, Inter Slovnaft (named after their petrol company sponsors) and Artmedia Bratislava who whooped Glasgow Celtic 5–0 in July 2005 in the Champions League qualifying stage. Founded in 1899, Artmedia was added to the team's name in 1993 to acknowledge the main sponsor,

an advertising agency. Slovan and Inter play near each other in the north of the city, whilst Artmedia come from the park just south of the Danube.

Artmedia Bratislava Krasovského 1; ☏ 02 6225 0043; www.fcartmedia.sk
AŠK Inter Slovnaft Vajnorská 100; ☏ 02 4437 1007; www.askinter.sk/futbal/index
ŠK Slovan Bratislava Junácka 2; ☏ 02 4437 3083; www.skslovan.sk

Golf
Bratislava Golf & Country Club at Bernolákovo; ☏ 02 5443 2008; www.golf.sk. The first golf course in Slovakia is found in the village of Bernolákovo, 16km east of Bratislava. Nine-hole course. Call in advance.
PKO Nábrežie arm gen Ľ. Svobodu 3; ☏ 02 5441 6040. ⊤ 1, 4, 5, 9, 12 or 17.

Hiking
See *Chapter 11* for some hiking trails.
See www.tanap.sk/hiking for hiking in High Tatras.

Horse racing
Zavodisko Bratislava race track Staroháska 29; ☏ 02 6224 6289; f 02 6231 5221; www.zavodisko.sk

Horseriding
Ranch at Podunajské Biskupice, Svornosti ulica 11; ☏ 02 4552 3051. Equestrian school, horseriding in the Slovak countryside.

Sports

Ice hockey

Slovan Bratislava are a world-beating team and Slovakia are ranked fourth in the world after Canada, Sweden and the Czech Republic (which must rankle). The home ice is at Odbojárov 9; ☏ 02 4437 2828.

Swimming pools

Hotel Danube See page 23. Has a good pool, open to the public. *Open Mon–Fri 10.00–12.00 & 14.00–22.00, Sat–Sun 14.00–18.00.*

Pasienky Pool Junácka 4. Two pools: 50m adult pool (*open Mon 19.30–22.00, Tue–Fri 06.00–07.30 & 19.30–22.00*) and 25m children's pool. Cost: adult 65Sk, child 35Sk. *Both pools open Sat–Sun 10.30–20.00.*

Zlaté Piesky Senecká cesta. Swim outside in summer in the large, soft-water lake. *Open daily 09.00–18.00.*

Summer bobsleigh run (Bobova dráha)

A popular destination is the bob track on Kamzík Hill. The track is 360m long, with 140m of that in the woods before emerging into a beautiful meadow. Rides are pretty speedy and descend 40m in altitude. *Summer opening times Mon–Fri 14.00–18.00, weekends 10.00–18.00.*

Tennis

The first Slovakian tennis courts were built in Bratislava between 1880 and 1890, where the game became popular with the elite classes. The first official tennis tournament was played in 1910. The 1988 Seoul Olympic gold medal-winner Miloslav Mečir has played a big part in popularising tennis in Slovakia; now they have ten men and ten women in the world top 100 rankings.

National Tennis Centre Prikopová 6; ☎ 02 4920 9888. Bratislava locals are very proud of their brand new sports hall. Voted Construction of the Year in 2003. Six tennis courts in a hall with a sliding roof.

Volleyball
PKO Nábrežie arm gen Ľ. Svobodu 3; ☎ 02 5441 6040. Check out www.volleyball.sk.

Shopping

It's never going to compete with Paris or Milan, but Bratislava probably doesn't want to. It's quite happy with what it's got.

There are swanky designer shops along Michalská and Ventúrska. Obchodná is the main shopping drag with teeny jeans shops and record stores with a growing number of shopping mall complexes situated a little out of the centre.

Take a cheap taxi (around € 10) out to see one of these mammoths. Polus City Centre, Shopping Park Bratislava, Shopping Park Soravia, the Aupark Shopping Mall and Avion Shopping Park, close to the airport are the pioneers of a mushrooming mall scene. Ikea and Tesco both have gigantic superstores out to the east of town near the spaghetti of ring roads and motorways. Tesco also has a crowded store on Kamenné námestie, right in the heart of town.

Polus City Center is out towards Zlaté Piesky and contains everything under the sun, plus restaurants, cafés, a cinema, bowling alley and other leisure facilities.

Aupark is within walking distance of the Old Town centre, a short hop across Nový most and hiding behind the greenery of Sad Janka Kráľa (park), at the beginning of the Petržalka housing estate. Aupark also has a range of facilities, numerous restaurants and cafés, a multiplex cinema and the like.

There are some fascinating speciality shops in Bratislava also, from quality wine shops to rare books. If you must have fur, you'll find none of that Western 'squeamishness' about draping a dead fox around your neck. Jewellery fans might pick up a bargain necklace here and there are some excellent outlets for fine art, ceramics, interior design and woodcrafts.

FOLK-ART CENTRES AND SOUVENIRS

There are many shops selling folk arts and crafts. The ÚĽuv centre for folk art production has a great selection of goods and gifts. ÚĽuv stands for Ústredie ľudovej umeleckej výroby (Centre for Folk Art Production) and has several outlets in Bratislava.

BKIS Klobučnícka 2; ☏ 02 5443 3715; e bkis@bkis.sk; www.bkis.sk. There is also a shop inside the BKIS office offering a range of maps, postcards, small folk crafts and books on Bratislava. *Open Mon–Fri 08.30–19.00, Sat–Sun 09.00–17.00.*

SOLID SERVICE

For some unusual little gifts to take home go to the courtyard of the Old Town Hall and there's an amazing elderly gentleman, Florián Takáč, selling metal Soviet badges, postcards, medals and military memorabilia from a tiny shop, Solidus. He's been there for ten years and obviously loves meeting people as he can converse in English, German, French, Italian, Russian, Spanish, Polish, Hungarian and Slovak. Now he's learning Japanese, 'So I can provide a better service.'

CHRISTMAS MARKET

Bratislava is the third city making up the triangle of great Austro-Hungarian cities (Budapest–Vienna–Bratislava). All three have wonderfully atmospheric and traditional Christmas fairs but Bratislava is possibly the most inviting. Bratislava has a beautifully renovated Old Town centre which is totally pedestrianised and thus perfect for tottering around after one too many mulled wines (to keep out the cold, of course) without fear of being mown down by a Škoda, careening across the icy roads.

The Bratislava Christmas market takes place from 26 November to 23 December in the twin main squares of the Old Town – Františkánske námestie and Hlavné námestie right in front of the Municipal Museum – and also on the graceful tree-lined square of Hviezdoslavovo námestie a few steps away. In December, the squares are packed with wooden booths

Shopping

Folk Folk Obchodná 10; ☏ 02/5443 4292
Folk Folk Rybáska brána 2; ☏ 02/5443 4874
ÚľŭV Michalská 4; ☏ 02/5443 2288
ÚľŭV Námestie SNP 12; ☏ 02/5292 3802
ÚľŭV Obchodná 64; ☏ 02/5273 1343; e craft@uluv.sk; www.uluv.sk
Suveníry Bratislavský hrad; ☏ 02/5934 1617

offering Christmas gifts, ornaments and a wide variety of festive food and drink. Dishes to try include *lokše* (potato pancakes) available with a choice of fillings, grilled meats such as *ciganska pečienka* (Gypsy cutlet), *langoše* (deep-fried doughnuts) or *chlieb mastou*, fresh bread smeared with lard and sprinkled with chopped onions, ideal for accompanying the mulled wine or the special Christmas punch drink. In 2005, the city commissioned the construction of new stalls inspired by the architecture of old Bratislava. Traders offer wooden toys, blown-glass ornaments, hand-painted pottery, Slovak folk art, beeswax candles and handmade gifts. Musical performances take place on a stage set up in front of the Municipal Museum and here you can also sample the special Slovak Christmas cabbage soup *kapustnica*, a delicious warming dish enhanced with homemade sausage, whipped cream and dried mushrooms.

Bratislava Shop Námestie SNP 13; ☎ 0905/158 242

FOOD AND DRINK
See also *Market values* box, page 147.
Čokoláda Michalska 6. With 60 kinds of hot chocolate.
Sv Urban Klobúčnicka. Quality wine shop.

Kodrianka Laurinská 4. Quality wine shop.

Vinotéka Trunk-Hurbanovo námestie 8. Wine shop.

Delvita In the Tatra Centrum, Hodžovo námestie 4. An excellent selection of Slovak wines and beers. *Open Mon–Fri 07.00–22.00, Sat–Sun 08.00–22.00.*

NEWSPAPERS, BOOKS, MAPS AND CDS

Steiner Antikvariat Michalská 20. Founded in 1847, ancient maps, ex-libris plates, second-hand books, etchings. Wonderful shop for browsing and fantasising about finding a treasure map. *Open Mon–Fri 10.00–18.00.*

ZMRZLINA – ICE-CREAM QUEUES

Sometimes Bratislava resembles Moscow in the 1980s, with people queuing for ice cream even in the depths of winter, but when the sun shines, the line is even longer.

Imaginative flavours include Bounty, After Eight, *punč* (fruit punch), *čoki*, nougat, coffee, *jahoda* (strawberry), *jablko* (apple), *citron* (lemon), *lieskove orechy* (hazelnut), *vanilka*, cappuccino, *banan* (very popular); also popular is one called *vitaminova* (it is bright orange and an elderly gentleman enquired whether it was made from carrots).

A scoop (*kopček* in Slovak) costs 8–10Sk; the cornet is thrown in too.

Slovensky Spisovatel Laurinská 2. Coffee-table books, maps, guides, literature.
Eurobooks Jesenského 5–9; ℡ 02 5441 7959; www.eurobooks.sk
Reduta Palackého 1; ℡ 02 5443 0203. Gorgeous coffee-table books.
Press International Obchodná 11
Kníhkupectvo Pištek Obchodná 2. Huge book store.
Svet Knihy Obchodná 4. Book shop with café.
Svetozor spol Štúrova 3. Coffee-table books on Slovakia.
CD shop Kollarovo námestie 20; www.musicmarket.sk. Music CDs cost between 200Sk and 1,000Sk.

Ice bar Luculus at Hviezdoslavovo námestie 19
Kafe Laguna at the corner of Laurinská and Ursulinska
Chicago 30s Club in front of the building on Námestie SNP (up by the partisan statue)
A **stand** on Kamenné námestie, in front of Tesco supermarket.
A **hole in the wall** in front of Coffee & Co at Obchodná 24 offers the bright orange vitaminova flavour

Pronouncing the word for ice cream should be first attempted only after consuming three half-litres of beer. Then, here we go: zrrrrmurrrzleeeeenah. See? No problem, now do it sober.

SHOPPING MALLS

Tesco Kamenné námestie

Aupark Shopping Center Einsteinova; www.aupark.sk

Polus City Center Vajnorska 100; www.poluscitycenter.sk

Danubia Shopping Centrum Panonska cesta 16/a, Petržalka

Hypermarket Tesco Panonska cesta 9, Petržalka

IKEA Ivanská cesta 18; ☏ 02 4341 2412; www.ikea.sk

Tatra Centrum Hodžovo námestie; www.tatracentrum.sk

Walking tours

WALK ONE – THE OLD TOWN

Estimated time: two hours

Bratislava is such an easy city to explore on foot but with its irregular shape and winding alleyways, a tour has to double back on itself, yet it's great because if you spot a church or an interesting-looking building you can be there in two minutes.

A good place to start is **Michalská veža** (Michael's Tower). This is also point zero and you can see the global distances to cities all around the world under the tower. Climb up five flights, observing the Museum of Historic Arms (page 209) on the way and you'll be rewarded with a great view of the 'little big city' as it now calls itself.

It's a magnificent panorama with the castle on one side, contrasting with the bizarre sight of a spaceship landing on the bridge. Back down again, on the right is **Baštová**, the narrowest alley in town and, in medieval times, home to the town's hangman. The streets of **Michalská** and **Ventúrska** are a continuation of each other and a good introduction to the town, lined with swanky shops and historic buildings. The largest building on Michalská is the former **Hungarian Chamber** built in 1756 and home to sessions of the Diet in the 19th century.

At the point where Michalská and Ventúrska meet you'll see a big rock with 'Korzo' written on it. This signals the start of the *korzo* or promenade, a custom that began with old Pressburg families and continues to this day as families stroll down towards the river in the evening. Further on, the **Zichy Palace** was built from 1770 to 1780 on the site of three medieval town houses. For a small town Bratislava is packed with palaces; near by Franz Liszt (aged nine) gave a concert in the garden pavilion of the **Leopold De Pauli Palace**. Just opposite, in the **Pálffy Palace** Mozart performed aged six, accompanied by his father, for the local aristocracy in 1762. It was the only concert he gave in the then Hungary.

The **Academia Istropolina** further along was founded in 1465 and at the time was the only university in Slovakia. On **Panská**, the **Keglevich Palace** was the scene of a concert by Beethoven. Babette Keglevich, the daughter of the count, was one of his students.

Head next for **St Martin's Cathedral** (page 223), scene of the coronation of 11 Hungarian kings and eight royal spouses. Look out for a gold model of the crown of Szent István, Hungary's first monarch, on top of the spire.

In **Rudnayovo námestie** there's a statue in molten metal with a Star of David on the top to commemorate the synagogue that stood here but was demolished to make way for the construction of the Nový most (New Bridge) in 1971.

Head back down Panská until you see a man's head poking out of a manhole. This is Čumil, one of the favourites of all the humorous works of art dotted around town. There are debates as to who he represents – whether a partisan or just a guy who likes to look up skirts. Turning left and we'll soon be on **Hlavné námestie**, site of endless pâtisseries (page 166) and perhaps a good place to relax for a while.

The yellow tower and red-roofed building opposite is the **Old Town Hall** (pages 223–4). Dating from the 15th century it came under fire when Napoleon attacked the city, a cannonball is still embedded in the wall. Apparently they fired from the other side of the river and so it must have been pretty powerful. The Jesuit church next door was built by the Lutherans in 1638 and on the king's wish it couldn't have a tower.

One of Napoleon's soldiers can still be found on the main square, leaning over the back of a bench, smiling smugly at the city he once helped to destroy. Follow the soldier's gaze and you arrive at the square's centrepiece, the **Roland Fountain**. Roland was a knight who was known as the protector of Bratislava and its citizens, yet the man on the top of the fountain is actually Maximillián II, the first Hungarian king to be crowned in Bratislava in the 16th century. After the town was ravaged by fire, Maximillián had the fountain built to provide water in case of future fires. According to one of the local legends, Maximillián rotates on top of the fountain once a year, at midnight on New Year's Eve, when he turns and salutes to all four directions. However, only female virgins can see him when he moves. Local wags say this phenomenon is rarely spotted because there are so few maidens left in the city.

You can walk through the Old Town courtyard to **Primaciálne námestie** where the **Primaciálny palác** (Primate's Palace) (page 225) is an explosion of pink and there's a black cardinal's hat on the tympanum. It's also worth going inside to see the hall of mirrors. The Hummel House just up the road celebrates the life of composer Johan Nepomuk Hummel.

From there it's a left, right, left through narrow streets and you'll find yourself out on **Hviezdoslavovo námestie**, a tongue-twisting square lined with trees and dominated by a statue to **Pavol Országh Hviezdoslav**, the 'father of Slovak poetry'. On the left is the neo-Renaissance **Slovenské narodné divadlo** (Slovak National Theatre), home to the opera. Over the square is the Reduta, home to the Slovak Philharmonic. The huge Buckingham-Palace-like building dominating the square is the Radisson SAS Carlton Hotel and there's a good coffee house inside for battery charging.

Walk down between the Reduta and the Carlton, passing the bizarre statue to patriot **Ľudovít Štúr** with figures suspended halfway up a pillar and you're out by the Danube.

Turn left and head towards the **Slovak National Museum** (page 211) guarded by a statue of a proud lion. Now it's going to be a short hike through a more urban landscape. Follow **Vajanského nábrežie** to the busy junction of **Šafárikovo námestie** and cross over. One block later turn left onto **Bezručova** and walk two blocks. Suddenly an amazing image comes into view: Budapest architect Ödön Lechner's incredible, almost edible **Blue Church** (*modrý kostolík*). The Art Nouveau church (page 226) dedicated to St Alžbeta looks like it's covered in blue icing and inside it's all blue too.

WALK TWO – THE CASTLE AND FURTHER AFIELD

Estimated time: three hours

This is going to be a bit more complicated and you'll need one tram ticket for a journey through the tunnel. Start off by negotiating the busy **Staromestská** main road which slices through the city and cuts off the Old Town from the castle. Begin at the **Clock Museum** (page 209) in the **Dom U Dobrého Pasteria** (House of the Good Shepherd), a tall yellow rococo whimsy. This area is the old Jewish quarter, what little remains of it. Walk up the steep **Beblavého**, which in the past was the city's red-light street and was visited by author Patrick Leigh Fermor on his walking journey to Constantinople. It's a steep climb up to **Bratislava Castle** (Bratislavský hrad) (page 222), dubbed the 'upside-down bedstead', but it's worth it for the view and the museum in the castle. There's also a good restaurant, Hradná vináren, in which to recuperate. The view is mixed as you can see the UFO café perched above the bridge but over the river the sprawling housing district of Petržalka is the stereotypical ugly eastern European image. The long concrete construction that you'll see over the river is **Incheba**, a massive convention and exhibition site. Over the river and to the right are the woods of Austria.

After a gentle stroll downhill and right following the base of Castle Hill, we come to a strange, foreboding black block which is the **memorial to Chatam Sofer**, the scholar and rabbi Mose Schreiber. If you're lucky the elderly custodian will be there and can show you round the underground Jewish cemetery (see page 209 for contact details).

Walk a little way upstream to catch the number 5 tram which will take you on a spooky ghost train ride under the castle to **Kapucínska**. It's good to get off at the first stop after the tunnel as there are some pretty churches to visit. Walk in the same direction along to **Hurbanovo námestie** where there is the **Church of St John of Matha**, one of the finest examples of Baroque architecture in Bratislava. Walk up **Suché mýto** (Dry toll) and we reach **Hodžovo námestie** and a view of the **Grassalkovich Palace** (page 226), a fine Rococo building

(page 226)

WHICH WITCH?

On Hurbanovo námestie at the place where you come out of Michalská brána onto the square there is a metal plaque set into the pavement commemorating the place where the first witch was burnt to death in Bratislava on 24 May 1602. (The building housing Woch restaurant on Františkanske námestie was home to the last woman burned at the stake in Bratislava for being a witch.)

Many of Slovakia's oldest seasonal traditions have their roots in ancient folklore and superstition. Between the end of November and the winter solstice, people believed that the powers of darkness, in the shape of witches and demons, held sway over the forces of good, drawing increased strength from the longer nights. The five main feast days during this period became known as the Witches' Days.

Walking tours

constructed in 1760, now home to the president. Behind is a spacious park where Slovaks enjoy the sun in their lunch hours. Further north is **Námestie Slobody** (page 220), home to what was supposedly the largest post office in the world although it's now mostly ministry offices. At the northern side of the square is the magnificent Baroque **Archbishop's Summer Palace** built in the second half of the 18th century by Viennese royal architect F A Hillebrandt. A little further along the street is the bizarre vision of Slovak Radio's inverted pyramid.

The first of these, **St Katarína's Day, 25 November**, marked the start of protecting oneself against malevolent forces. Villagers ate a lot of garlic to ward off evil spirits and even fed it to their livestock. If the first visitor on 25 November was a woman then the crockery was in danger of smashing all year.

The last and most significant witch day was **St Lucia's Day, 13 December**. For some countries she is the 'saint with beautiful eyes', the patron saint of light and curer of eye diseases, while others claim she was the greatest witch of all time. Some claim she could not be burnt at the stake. At the stroke of midnight on St Lucia's Day, villagers believed they could peer through the keyhole of the local church and identify all the witches in the village. It was also important to eat a lot of garlic on this day.

If you have any energy left, I suggest walking towards the Danube over Nový most (New Bridge) and taking the lift up to the UFO café for a drink, a meal and a spectacular view. Then walk back downstream in the **Sad Janka Kráľa** (park), a lovely green space, and return to the northern side by the railway bridge.

UFO café

Museums and sightseeing

10

MUSEUMS

Bratislava is packed with museums and there is a great variety of themes, from wine to cars, from dungeons to clocks. Everyone will find something to entertain them on a rainy Wednesday afternoon. Museums in Bratislava are almost always open from 10.00 to 17.00 and always closed on Monday.

Unmissables

Arms and fortifications (and panoramic view) Michael's Gate/Tower; Michalská 24; ☎ 02 5443 3044 [1 B2]

Five floors of weapons and armour then a great view of the city from the top. Adult 40Sk, child 20Sk. *Open Tue–Sun 10.00–17.00.*

Chatam Sofer Memorial Nabrežie arm gen Ľ. Svobodu [4 A6]

A Jewish cemetery was buried underground when the road level was raised in 1942. It contains 23 graves including that of Chatam Sofer, a great scholar, also known as rabbi Mose Schreiber. The guide, Juraj Kohlmann, doesn't always stay at the memorial as he gets cold, but you can call for an appointment on his cell phone at 0903 221 842. US$2 for tourists, Jews come to pray at no charge. *Open Mon–Fri 09.00–17.00.*

Clocks Museum (Expozicia Historickych Hodin) Židovska 1; Dom U Dobrého Pastiera' (House of the Good Shepherd); ☎ 02 5441 1940 [1 A3]

Clocks and watches made in Bratislava when it was Pressburg. Also combined with the Exhibition of Crafts just over the road on Beblavého ulica. Adult 50Sk, child 20Sk; one ticket for two museums. *Open Oct–Apr; Tue–Sun 09.30–16.00; May–Sep Tue–Fri 10.00–17.00, Sat–Sun 11.00–18.00.*

History of Bratislava (and feudal justice in cellar) Old Town Hall, Primaciálne námestie 1 [1 C2/3]
Under the Municipal Museum (see below) and with the same entry ticket this is a great little museum. Children will love the gruesome dungeons and torture equipment. *Open Tue–Fri 10.00–17.00, Sat–Sun 11.00–18.00.*

Municipal Museum (Mestské múzeum) Primaciálne námestie 1; ℡ 02 5443 1473; www.muzeumbratislava.sk [1 C2/3]
Massive museum with a series of seemingly endless rooms. The history of Bratislava is shown and some of the rooms have the original furnishings. Interesting collection of pub signs. Adults 50Sk, concessions 20SK. *Open Tue–Sun 10.00–18.00.*

Museum at Devín Castle Muránska ulica, Bratislava-Devín; ℡ 02 6573 0105
B̲ 29 from Nový most
Ruined castle on a crag above the Danube (see *Beyond the city*, page 228). Devín Castle entry: adult 60Sk, concessions 20Sk. *Open Tue–Sun 10.00–17.00, May–Sep Sat–Sun 10.00–19.00 also.*

Museum of Jewish Culture Židovska 17; ☏ 02 5441 8507;
www.slovak-jewish-heritage.org/mblava.htm [4 A6]
The museum is housed in the late Renaissance 17th-century Zsigray Mansion on the
side of Castle Hill by the tram tunnel. The moving exhibition features the history and
culture of Jews living in the territory of Slovakia since the times of the Great
Moravian Empire. It shows the everyday life of the Jewish community, synagogue
furnishings, important Jews in Slovakia's history, as well as a harrowing section on the
Holocaust. Adult 200Sk, child 60Sk, photo permit 100Sk. *Open Sun–Fri 11.00–17.00.*

**Slovak National Museum/History Museum at Bratislava Castle (Historické
Múzeum)** Bratislava Castle, Mudroňova 1; ☏ 02 5934 1626; www.snm-hm.sk [1 A3]
A collection of exhibitions on three floors of the castle with silver treasures,
antique furniture, arms and armour. Climb up three flights of grey marble to the
cash desk, then even higher to the Crown Tower where you can go up a
Hitchcockian stairway to the top of one of the four towers. Adult 80Sk, child 40Sk.
Separate ticket for the Treasury: adult 20Sk, child 10Sk. *Open Tue–Sun 09.00–17.00.*

Slovak National Museum-Natural Science Museum (Prírodovedné Múzeum)
Vajanského nábrežie 2; ☏ 02 5934 9122; f 02 5296 6653; www.snm.sk [1 D4]
On the top floor are two temporary exhibitions: maps and eagles. On the second
floor is a permanent exhibit of the flora and fauna of Slovakia, with animals
presented in naturalistic settings, clever optical illusions of painted backdrops to give
a sense of space, a lot of rocks too. On the first floor is Slovak culture, also very

interesting. On the ground floor is a temporary exhibition space which continues into the café at the back. Adults 60Sk, concessions 40Sk. *Open Tue–Sun 09.00–18.00.*

Wine and viticulture (Vinohradícke museum) Radničná ulica 1; ☏ 02 5443 1743 [1 C3]

The history of viticulture in Slovakia for over 2,000 years in a well-presented exhibition. Adult 50Sk, child 20Sk. *Open May–Sep Tue–Fri 10.00–17.00, Sat–Sun 11.00–18.00, Oct–Apr Tue–Sun 09.30–16.30.*

Other museums

Archaeological Museum Žižkova 2; ☏ 02 5441 6034 [4 A6]

In a 16th-century Renaissance building the museum features temporary exhibitions of artefacts from prehistoric times until the late Middle Ages. Adult 20Sk, concessions 10Sk. *Open Tue–Sun 09.00–17.00.*

Musical exhibition House of J N Hummel, Klobučnícka ulica 2; ☏ 02 5443 3888 [1 C2]

The museum is in the little peach-coloured cottage where pianist and composer Hummel was born. There is a shop selling CDs too. Adult 40Sk, child 20Sk. *Open Mon–Fri 10.00–18.00, Sat 10.00–14.00. (Lunch break 11.45–12.30 daily.)*

Museum Arthur Fleischman Biela 6; ☏ 02 5443 4742 [1 B2]

The family of pioneering sculptor Fleischman lived in this building in the Old Town. The museum is upstairs above a peaceful courtyard with old stone fountain. Adult 40Sk, child 20Sk. *Open Tue–Fri 10.00–17.00, Sat–Sun 11.00–16.00.*

Museum of Culture of Carpathian Germans Žižkova 14; ⏍ 02 5441 5570;
f 02 5441 5570; e muzeumkkn@stonline.sk [4 A6]
Showing the craftsmanship of ethnic Germans in Slovakia: enamel, glass, porcelain,
jewellery. Adult 40Sk, concessions 20Sk. *Open Tue–Sun 10.00–16.00.*

Museum of Hungarian Culture in Slovakia (Múzeum Kultúry Maďarov na
Slovensku) Brämerova kúria, Žižkova 18; ⏍ 02 5441 2021; f 02 5441 2023;
e mkms@snm.sk [4 A6]
Set in a 16th-century Renaissance building, and featuring details of Hungarian life
with photos and ethnographic artefacts. There are 530,000 Hungarians living in
Slovakia. Adult 40Sk, concessions 20Sk. *Open Tue–Sun 10.00–17.00.*

Museum of Transport (Múzeum Dopravy) Šancová ulica 1; ⏍ 02 5244 4163;
f 02 5249 4021; e muzeumdophravy@slovanet.sk; www.muzeumdopravy.com
More than 80 cars and 35 motorbikes make this a fun afternoon and there's the
history of road and rail transport. Near the main railway station. Adult 40Sk,
concessions 20Sk. *Open Tue–Fri 10.00–16.00, Sat–Sun 10.00–17.00.*

Múzeum Antická Gerulata Gerulatská ulica 69, Rusovce; ⏍ 02 6285 9332
B̲ *91 from Nový most heading towards Čuňovo.*
In Rusovce, archaeologists uncovered the foundations of a Roman military camp
dating from AD100–400. Roof tiles, bricks, sculptures, tombstones and daily
household items made of bronze and iron. Adult 30Sk, child 20Sk. *Open Tue–Fri
10.00–17.00, May–Oct open also Sat–Sun 10.00–18.00.*

Museums

GALLERIES
The Unmissables

Mirbach Palace (Mirbachov Palác) Františkánske námestie 11; ☎ 02 5443 1556; f 02 5443 2611; www.gmb.sk/en/mirbachov_palac [1 C2]
Like the Pálffy Palace (below), the Mirbach's interior is a match for the exhibits. Two of the rooms are lined with amazing wooden panels showing scenes of aristocratic life created in 1704–80. There are 290 prints with oak border under glass. Adults 80Sk, concessions 40Sk. *Open Tue–Sun 11.00–18.00.*

Pálffy Palace (Pálffyho Palác) Panská 19; ☎ 02 5443 3627; www.gmb.sk/en/palffyho_palac.html [1 B3]
A fascinating gallery where the interior is probably more interesting than the exhibits. Also features an amazing permanent exhibit by Slovak artist Matej Krén called *Pasáž* where visitors walk along a visual gangplank through a seemingly endless library of bookshelves. Not for those with vertigo; unsettling yet fascinating. Adult 60Sk, concessions 30Sk. *Open Tue–Sun 11.00–18.00.*

Primate's Palace (Primaciálny palác) Primaciálne námestie 1; ☎ 02 5935 6111; www.gmb.sk/en/primacialny_palac.html [1 C2]
Pink wedding-cake exterior, tapestries from Mortlake, London, and the Hall of Mirrors where they signed the Pressburg Peace Treaty in 1805 between Napoleon and Holy Roman Emperor Francis II of Austria. Adults 40Sk, children and students (with card) free. *Open Tue–Sun 10.00–17.00.*

ART NOUVEAU IN BRATISLAVA

Several examples of Art Nouveau in a very Baroque city are:

Blue Church by Ödön Lechner, 1910–13 (pages 226–7) [1 E3]
High school around the corner at Grösslingova 18 also by Ödön Lechner, 1906–08 [1 E2]
Stained-glass atrium ceiling in post office on Námestie SNP 34 [1 C2]. Wachtler Palace was built in 1778 but its original appearance is known only from photographs. The city bought the palace from its owners, counts Szápáry and Pallavicini, to move the management of the post office there. The original Wachtler Palace was pulled down in 1908 to give way to the building that is now the Old Post Office. Its construction was finished in 1912 and the designer was the architect Gyula Partos from Budapest.
Hlavné námestie Magyar Bank, built 1908 by R Körösym, now Roland Café [1 C2]
House on Štúrova ulica built in 1903 by Jozef Schiller [1 D/E3]
Roland Café Art Nouveau bank originally. Hlavne námestie 5 [1 C3]. (Home to a copy of Kempelen's chess robot – see page 224.)
Šafárikovo námestie – townhouse on corner built in 1904 by Jozef Schiller [1 E4]

Slovak National Gallery Razusovo nábrežie 2; ☏ 02 5443 2082; www.sng.sk [1 C4]
Exhibition of Gothic art, Baroque art in Slovakia, 19th-century art and religious art but the best thing are the 12 'character heads' by František Xaver Messerschmidt (1736–83). He was a talented woodcarver and you can play a guessing game as to what expression is on each grimacing head: sanctimoniousness? gormlessness? smugness? Adult 80Sk, concessions 40Sk. *Open Tue–Sun 10.00–17.30.*

Other galleries
Bibiana Panská 41; ☏ 02 5443 1388; www.bibiana.sk [1 C3]
International house of art for children with all kinds of events: art, theatre, performance, exhibitions and books. Admission free. *Open Tue–Sun 10.00–18.00.*

Galleria 'Medium' Hviezdoslavovo námestie 18; ☏ 02 5443 5334 [1 B3]
Exhibition space for the students of the Academy of Fine Art and Design. Voluntary donations. *Open Tue–Sun 10.00–17.00 Thu 12.00–17.00.*

Umelka Dostojevského rad 2 [1 E4]
Exhibition space of the Slovak Union of Visual Arts (Slovenská výtvarná únia). An excellent place for exhibiting: one bright roomy hall with adventurous works and installations. Next to the Umelka pub. Admission free. *Open Tue–Sun 11.00–17.00.*

GARDENS AND PARKS
Bratislava is a very green city. There are 809ha of parks and forests and 34 protected reservations. Most of this is formed by the **Bratislava Forest Park**

(Bratislavský lesov park) to the north of the city. The hills above the city make an excellent cool getaway from the heat of the summer city. The hills are criss-crossed with hiking trails and cycle paths. Here are a few places to get some oxygen.

Botanical Garden (Botanická Záhrada), Botanická 3; ☏ 02 6542 5440;
www.uniba.sk/bzuk/e_index.htm
T̄ 1, 4, 5, 9, 12 to Botanická Záhrada stop
The 5ha Botanical Garden contains more than 5,000 species of exotic and domestic plants and 650 woodland species. Established in 1942, the garden became an important centre for botanical study only after World War II, when scientists working at the Comenius University undertook much research work there. Adult 40Sk, child 20Sk, annual season ticket 200Sk. *Open 1 April–31 Oct daily 09.00–18.00, greenhouses open 09.00–15.00, 1 Nov–31 Mar Mon–Fri 09.00–15.00.*

Bratislava Zoo Mlynská dolina 1, 842 27 Bratislava; ☏ 02 6542 2848, f 02 6542 1868; email zoo@zoobratislava.sk; www.zoobratislava.sk
B̄ 30, 31, 32, 37, 39, 92
A modest zoo park set up in the hills to the west of town. Hippos, bears, monkeys, lemurs all in a hilly park. Adult 60Sk (winter), 99Sk (summer), children and concessions 40Sk (winter), 59Sk (summer). *Open daily 10.00–15.00 winter, 09.00–18.00 summer.*

Gardens and parks

HUMOROUS STATUES – AMUSING, CREEPY OR JUST PLAIN WEIRD

Napoleonic army soldier leaning on bench in Hlavné námestie [1 C3]

Čumil – man peering out of manhole cover 'looking up skirts' by Viktor Hulík [1 C3]

Photographer peering around corner by Paparazzi restaurant – who designed it. Fits in well with restaurant theme. [1 C3]

Schöne Náci – a real dandy, Ignác Lamár. This is Schöne Náci, which means 'Handsome Ignazius'. In fact, he was a real person who was locally famous for strolling the Korzo (a promenade stretching from Michalská brána to Hviezdoslav Square). He appears quite friendly and jolly, but he was actually somewhat

Grassalkovich Gardens (Grassalkovichova záhrada) [2 D2/3]

Situated behind Grassalkovich Palace, the official residence of the Slovak president, this is a rather formal garden with little shade. Along the side are trees planted by visiting dignitaries and royalty. People are not supposed to walk on the grass or bring the dog but it's pleasant enough for a stroll. *Open daily 09.00–19.00 (17.00 in winter).*

disturbed because of a trauma he experienced. Schöne Náci had a fiancée before German troops came in World War II, but she was deported to a Nazi concentration camp where she died. He never recovered mentally from this and he never married. He just strolled the Korzo and smiled and ate his cake in the shops, and then died completely forgotten. His grave can be found in Lehnice (a small village halfway between Bratislava and Dunajská Streda, on highway 572).

Skateboarder girls – Poštova and Obchodná – one sitting on fence, one below on skateboard looking up [1 C1]

Posmievačik – the Mocker A grotesque gargoyle from a late Gothic façade. Horrible dwarf squatting with genitals out at Panská 29. Various theories about his significance. Some say he is looking towards Vidrica, the red-light district and that's why he is aroused. Others say he represents a very nosy resident of the building who likes to spy on passers-by from a tiny bay window. [1 B3]

Horský Park

Situated to the northwest of town, the 20ha Horský Park is a woody area with a network of paths. There is a gamekeeper's lodge in the middle which is a popular destination and also a 'Lourdes cave' with a Kalvária pilgrimage site founded in 1694 by the Jesuits, the city council and the archbishop who decided to build it in the same place as where the Turkish guards had stood in the time of their raids.

Medical Garden (Medická Záhrada) [3 G/H3]

A pleasant park to the northeast of the city where people take their lunch break, walk the dog or play frisbee. There's a children's playground at one side and a statue to the Slovak writer Martin Kukučin by the Croatian sculptor Ivan Meštrovic. The garden once belonged to the palace of Gobert, Count of Aspremont which stands next to the park. It is a late Baroque palace in a delicate pink hue, commissioned in 1769. Later, the palace was owned by the Esterházy family. Jozef Haydn gave concerts at the palace. After the Great War the palace became the property of Comenius University medical department. *Open daily 09.00–19.00 (17.00 in winter).*

Námestie Slobody Park [2 E2]

On one side it claimed to feature the largest post office in the world although these days the imposing building is occupied by the Ministry of Transportation, Post and Telecommunications while one resident, the giant statue of former communist president, Klement Gottwald, has been removed. A modern statue of a giant metal flower rises up in the centre. On the side opposite the post office is the Technical College and there are some great Soviet constructivist reliefs all along the wall, with groups of happy workers, bucolic peasants and clever-looking scientists.

Sad Janka Kráľa [4 D/E8, 5 F8]

South of the Danube, this park seems like the first choice for those seeking a patch of green. The park was created in the time of Maria Theresa. Kráľa was a revolutionary poet who used to walk there. There are several features of interest in the park and several restaurants. You can find a statue of revolutionary Hungarian poet Sándor Petôfi who lived in Bratislava for a while and also a 14th-century Franciscan church tower which used to stand in the Old Town but was removed from the church and brought to the park in 1897. The football ground of Artmedia Bratislava, 2005 champions, is towards the southern end of the park while the ground-breaking Aréna Theatre stands by the water.

Slavín monument [2 B1]

Situated up a well-to-do residential part of town to the northwest, Slavín Hill is crowned with a memorial to the 6,850 Soviet soldiers who lost their lives in the battle for Bratislava. The graves lie in a quiet garden and there are some interesting heroic statues by Tibor Bartfay. A 37m-high column also by Bartfay has a soldier raising a flag and a gold star on the top. Around the base of the monument are the names of the Slovak towns and the dates they were 'liberated' by the Red Army. At one side there is a peace garden instigated by Alexander Dubček. There is a great view of the city and it seems huge with many more skyscrapers and tower blocks than other

Gardens and parks

'eastern' cities in the region. It's easy to find as Slavín is visible from all parts of town and you just head off uphill through a district of villas with interesting architectural styles.

MAJOR SIGHTS
Bratislava Castle (Bratislavský hrad) [1 A3, 4 B5/6]

Today described somewhat cruelly as an 'upside-down bedstead' or an 'upturned table', Bratislava Castle was first constructed in a more basic fortress style in 1430 by King Sigismund of Luxembourg. There had been previous fortifications on the site, Celts and Romans had occupied the hill, then in the 9th century the Slavs built a fort on the hill which rises 85m above the Danube. The conquering Magyars also built fortifications on the hill and there was extensive construction work in the 13th century. King Sigismund reconstructed the castle and added outer defence walls, some 11m thick. The Habsburgs used the castle as protection when the Turks attacked Vienna. It received its trademark four corner towers between 1635 and 1649 when the Hungarian Viceroy Pál Pálffy called in Giovanni Battista Carlone to help. Maria Theresa called it 'her castle' and the Hungarian crown jewels were kept there when the capital of Hungary was moved to Bratislava and she converted it into a grand palace in 1761. The interior was redesigned in a lavish Rococo style and a number of annexes were added on outside. Maria Theresa's successors did not share her love for the castle and it fell into disrepair. It was used for a while as a priests' seminary and a barracks. In 1811 it burnt down in a devastating fire and remained in ruin for 140 years until restoration work began in 1953. Today it houses exhibitions for the Slovak National Museum as well as state rooms of the Slovak National Council.

St Martin's Cathedral (Dóm sv Martina) [1 B3, 4 D6]

Building work on the three-aisled church lasted from the 13th to the middle of the 15th century. Between 1563 and 1830 it was the coronation church for the kings of Hungary and witnessed the crowning of 11 Hungarian kings and eight royal spouses. The tower is 85m tall and is topped with a 300kg gilded model of the crown of St Stephen, the first king of Hungary (in AD 1000). The late Gothic vaulting is by Hans Puchspaum under direct influence of master masons from Vienna. When in residence, the archbishop of Esztergom invited a famous sculptor to the Austrian court, Georg Raphael Donner, to Bratislava to establish a workshop and Donner stayed 11 years creating many masterpieces. In 1734 he created a new high altar featuring an equestrian statue of *St Martin and the Beggar* which now stands in the southeast corner of the nave and from 1732 to 1734 built the chapel of St John the Almsgiver in the north aisle with the kneeling figure of the donor, the Archbishop Esterházy. In 1884 Franz Liszt conducted his *Coronation Mass* here.

Old Town Hall (Stará radnica) [1 C2/3, 4 E5]

Right in the heart of Hlavné námestie (Main Square) is the Old Town Hall with its distinctive yellow tower and red roof. It was developed in the 14th century from a

Major sights

group of houses belonging to the mayors of the city to form the unusual conglomeration of styles and colours known as the 'House with the Tower'. The rib-vaulted late Gothic passage leads to a beautiful courtyard with Renaissance arcades. Following a fire in 1733 the tower was restored in the Baroque style. The tower has a cannonball embedded in the wall from the time of the Napoleonic attacks; the cannons fired from across the river. Inside, the 14th-century Gothic chapel was restored in 1969. It can be visited as it forms part of the Municipal Museum.

THE AMAZING TURK – KEMPELEN'S CHESS 'MACHINE'

See a model (not working) in Roland coffee house on Hlavné námestie.

Wolfgang von Kempelen, the inventor of the Magic Turk chess-playing automaton, was born in Bratislava in 1734 (died 1804) in the building to the left of the university library.

In 1770, The Turk made its first appearance in front of the Viennese court. On a signal from the Empress Maria Theresa, Baron Wolfgang von Kempelen slowly wheeled his creation forward. The 1m-high wooden cabinet with a large chessboard screwed to its top ran on four brass casters that not only allowed it to move freely, but also raised it slightly off the floor so that the audience could see that there was nothing hiding underneath. Behind the box sat a figure, dressed in oriental clothing and a bulky turban. Kempelen challenged

Primate's Palace (Primaciálny palác) [1 C2]

The powder-pink neo-Classical palace was built between 1777 and 1781 by Melchior Hefele for Cardinal József Batthyányi, Archbishop of Esztergom and Primate of Hungary who used it as his winter palace. The tympanum on the roof features a mosaic based on a fresco by Franz Anton Maulpertsch and right on the top is a 150kg cast-iron black cardinal's hat. The palace has a collection of tapestries from Mortlake, London. The Hall of Mirrors was the scene of the signing of the

audience members to play the Turk at chess. Almost all were defeated. During its tours, the Turk fascinated Napoleon, Benjamin Franklin, Edgar Allan Poe and computing pioneer Charles Babbage.

The chess player was, in fact, destined to become the most famous automaton in history. And along the way, Kempelen's work would unwittingly help to inspire the development of the power loom, the telephone, the computer, and the detective story.

In 1766 Kempelen was appointed director of the imperial salt mines in Transylvania. He devised a system of pumps to drain the mines when they became flooded with water. Following the success of this project, he was asked to design the waterworks for Bratislava Castle. He devised a pump to carry water up to the castle from the Danube, as before that all they had was one well.

Major sights

'Peace of Pressburg' treaty between Napoleon and Emperor Francis I on 26 December 1805 after the Battle of Austerlitz.

Grassalkovich Palace (Grassalkovičov palác) [2 D3]

Built from 1760 to 1765 as a summer residence for Count Anton Grassalkovitch, the president of the Hungarian Royal Chamber, the Baroque palace stands in an open space north of the Old Town and behind there is a French-style garden. The architect of the project was Mayerhoffer. Grassalkovitch was an influential man and later became advisor to Empress Maria Theresa. In the 18th century, the palace was a meeting place for members of the Hungarian aristocracy. The palace today serves as the residence for the president of Slovakia.

The Blue Church (Modrý kostolík) [1 E3, 5 G5]

The full title is the Church of St Elizabeth. In 1907, it was the 700th anniversary of the birth of St Elizabeth (sv Alžbeta). Elizabeth, the daughter of Endre II of Hungary, was born in Bratislava and was the city's only well-known saint. It was decided that a church be built in her honour and permission was asked from the Hungarian Archbishop Vászáry. The Hungarian architect and 'father of Hungarian Art Nouveau' Ödön Lechner was commissioned to design a church while Antal Durvay was in charge of the construction work. Lechner used concrete for the church and covered the exterior with plaster painted in several shades of blue, decorated with ceramic floral tiles in darker blue. Lechner knew the legend of St Elizabeth (see box

THE LEGEND OF ST ELIZABETH

St Elizabeth spent all her time looking after and feeding the poor and needy. She built a hospital at the foot of the mountain where her castle stood and tended the sick against her family's wishes. Once, when she was taking bread to the ailing poor, her husband, Prince Louis of Thuringa, stopped her and asked to look under her apron to see if she was carrying roses, as she claimed. When he lifted the apron the bread had been miraculously changed to roses.

above) well and he used the rose motif many times in the decoration. Budapest painter Gyula Tury painted the altar showing Elizabeth giving alms to the poor outside Wartburg Castle. The church was consecrated on 11 October 1913.

11

Beyond the city

DEVÍN

$\overline{\text{B}}$ *29 from Nový most*

Devín is considered a vital part of Slovak history and it's an impressive sight when you arrive, probably by bus or boat, to see it rising up on a tall crag above the confluence of the Danube and Morava rivers. Dating from Roman times, a palace was added in the 15th century, and for a time it belonged to the notorious Báthory family (Erzsébet was the 'Blood Countess'). In 1809, Napoleon's advancing troops blew up the fortress en route to a confrontation with Habsburg forces. It later became a central symbol for the Slovak National Revival and Ľudovít Štúr organised a series of events to whip up national fervour. In summer you can also take a ferry across to Hainburg so don't forget your passport (adults €5, children €3). Walking around you'll discover hiking routes, cycle routes and even a lighthouse. Also if you follow the road around, there's a wonderful outdoor grill restaurant, Pizzeria Istria, with grilled fish, garlic sausages and jars of pickled chilli peppers. Devín Castle entry: adult 60Sk, concessions 20Sk. *Open Tue–Sun 10.00–17.00, May–Sep Sat–Sun 10.00–19.00 also.*

CYCLE ROUTES

Slovakia is an appealing destination for the adventure traveller and the Carpathian and Tatra mountain ranges provide good terrain for walking and trekking.

Europe's longest cycling route passes through Slovakia, stretching from Passau in Germany along the Danube, through Vienna, Bratislava and on to Štúrovo. Cyclists can then continue their journey by taking a ferry across the Danube into Hungary. There is a very good network of marked trails in all mountain areas.

Cycle route 8km from the Karlova Ves, or along Morava, from Devinska Nova Ves (4.5km). There is a special cycling route, which is a part of the informational pathway at the Morava River floodplain.

The tracks in Petržalka are linked to the cycle paths in Austria, leading along the embankment to the quaint town of Hainburg, which is at the crossroads of two interesting long-distance European hiking and cycling routes.

KAMZÍK

🚎 *203 from Hodžovo námestie*
The best-known part of Bratislava Forest Park is north of the city underneath the TV tower. Kamzík Hill (439m) offers cool woods and a range of trails to follow at the southernmost tip of the Small Carpathian mountain range. There are little triangular wooden huts, looking like chunks of Toblerone, offering draught beer or *Kofola* (a local version of Coca-Cola) on tap. At the top is a huge meadow where locals can ski in winter, nicknamed *Cvicna luka* (training meadow). In summer, a bobsleigh run follows the slope for 360m with ten bends, one jump and one crossing. The 200m-high tower has a revolving Veža restaurant and café at the top (see pages 165 & 168). Koliba Expo is a restaurant resembling a traditional log cabin, presently undergoing reconstruction.

Kamzík

ZLATÉ PIESKY

T̄ 2 or 4

In the heat of the summer, Bratislava residents head off on the tram to Golden Sands, Zlaté Piesky, a 32ha artificial lake surrounded by campsites and stalls offering snacks. Even the roar of the main road nearby can't deter families from having fun, splashing about in the soft, clear waters of the lake. It also has an excellent and very popular restaurant. It has a little of a socialist-era children's camp about it but it's worth a trip to go to U Zlatého Vodnika (see *Eating and drinking*, page 165). Intercamp and Autocamp Zlaté Piesky (see *Camping section* of *Accommodation*, page 142) are two campsites at the 54ha lake resort where small cabins can be rented. The site also has a capacity of 300 pitches for tents and trailers.

DANUBIANA MEULENSTEEN ART MUSEUM

Vodne dielo, Čuňovo; ☏ 02 6252 8501; www.danubiana.sk

B̄ 91 from Nový most to Čuňovo, 15km south of Bratislava, then walk for about 3km following the signposts for the museum

An interesting and unusual modern art museum on the Danube bank. The blue-and-white building looks like a ship and it's the brainchild of Vincent Polakovič who decided to create the museum after an encounter with the ghost of his hero, Vincent van Gogh. A Dutch millionaire put up US$1 million to fund the project. While you're in Čuňovo you can see the dam system and the controversial Gabčikovo water project 40km downstream. The area is a centre of wild-water sports, slalom and rafting events. Museum entry: adults 60Sk, concessions 30Sk. *Open May–Sep Tue–Sun 10.00–20.00, Oct–Apr Tue–Sun 10.00–18.00.*

ČERVENÝ KAMEŇ

The name means 'red rock' and it's an impressive 13th-century castle with spectacular cellars (the largest in central Europe), a massive cavernous hall that held wine for the Fugger family and subsequent nobility such as the Palffys. The castle is only 30km from Bratislava and the best way to see it is on a tour. The BKIS (Bratislava Tourist Service; *Klobučnićka 2;* ℡ *02 5443 4059, 02 5443 1707;* f *02 5443 2708;* e *info@bkis.sk*) arranges tours of the local area and provides guides (in 13 languages) for walking and sightseeing. The Small Carpathian Wine Route trip usually combines a visit to the ceramics factory in Modra, and visits to wine-producing villages like Pezinok.

The main railway station *(Hlavná stanica)* is out to the north of the city; tram number 1 takes you there. The main bus station (*autobusová stanica*) is out to the east at Mlynské Nivy 31 [3 K4], a short taxi ride from the centre or bus 88 from Nový most.

Language

More than five million people speak Slovak in Slovakia and a few million more abroad. However, it hasn't all been plain sailing, or speaking, for the Slovaks.

In AD863, Greek missionary brothers Cyril and Methodius came from Thessaloniki at the invitation of the Great Moravian Prince Rastislav. They came to Great Moravia and created the Old Church Slavonic alphabet, the origins of today's Cyrillic alphabet. They also translated liturgical books into Old Church Slavonic.

Pastor's son and national hero Ľudovít Štúr codified the Slovak literary language in 1843; before that, everything written down was in Czech.

Slovaks also had a hard time preserving their language as they were dominated for years by Hungarians and Austrians, both speaking, and forcing Slovaks to speak, languages with entirely different grammatical make-ups.

Slovak is a member of the Slavic group of languages, a large family including Russian, Ukrainian, Polish, Czech, Serbian, Croat and Slovenian, all of which have a devilish selection of possible endings, genders, declensions, conjugations and diacritical accents.

The Slovak vocabulary is about half that of English (approximately 220,000 words to English's 450,000).

Slovak is not as tricky to pronounce as Czech and less tiring for the tongue. It doesn't have the horrendous Czech 'ř' for a start. Having said that, neither is a doddle. However, a few choice phrases will not only endear you to the locals but also help decipher some of the tongue-twisting vowel-less words that litter Bratislava's streets. Try saying *zmrzlina* (see box *Zmrzlina – ice-cream queues*, page 198) after a few world-beating beers and you'll be amazed how easy it appears when wearing one's beer goggles. Good luck! (*Veľa šťastia!*)

PRONUNCIATION

Once you learn the rules, pronunciation is not so difficult as, unlike English, there are no peculiar irregularities in how you say what you see.

The vowels a, e, i, o, u are pure sounds, more like Spanish or Italian than English. Vowels can be either short (*a, ä, e, i, o, u, y*) or long (*á, é, í, ó, ú, ý*), basically pronounced with more emphasis, but keeping the same sound. Those consonants not included (*b, d, f, g, l, m, n, s, v, z*) can be pronounced as in English, with the exception of q and w which don't exist in Slovak except in some foreign words and names. The consonants *k, p* and *t* are as in English but not so aspirated.

a	as in **ah**
á	as in k**ar**ma
ä	as in h**ay**
c	like 'ts' in oats
č	like 'ch' in cheeky
ď	like 'dy' as in duty, *d* followed by *e* or *i* is also softened
dz	like 'ds' in heads

Pronunciation

dž	like 'j' in jam
e	as in b**e**d
é	as in th**ere**
ě	like the 'ye' in yes
h	quite breathily
ch	like 'ch' in Scottish 'loch'
i/y	as in spaghett**i**
í/ý	as in bel**ie**ve
j	like 'y' in yes
ľ	pronounced 'ly' like the *l* in lurid
ĺ	a long, long 'l' emphasised
ň	pronounced 'ny' like the *n* in **n**ewt, *n* followed by *e* or *i* is softened
o	as in h**o**t
ó	as in t**oe**
ö	pronounced 'ur'
ô	as in wh**oah**
r	rolled, as in a Scottish accent
ř	very rolled (but not followed by a *ž* in the scary Czech version)
š	'sh' as in shandy
ť	pronounced 'ty' as in **t**una, *t* followed by *e* or *i* is softened
u	as in r**oo**t
ú	as in sch**oo**l

Language

ů	pronounced more like a French 'u' with pouty lips
w	only found in foreign words and pronounced as a 'v' (WC is *vay-tsay*)
ž	like the 's' in lei**s**ure

WORDS AND PHRASES
Numbers

0	*nula*	5	*päť*	10	*desať*
1	*jeden*	6	*šesť*	20	*dvadsať*
2	*dva*	7	*sedem*	100	*sto*
3	*tri*	8	*osem*	1,000	*tisíc*
4	*štyri*	9	*deväť*	2006	*dvetisíc šesť*

Days of the week

Monday	*pondelok*	Friday	*piatok*
Tuesday	*utorok*	Saturday	*sobota*
Wednesday	*streda*	Sunday	*nedeľa*
Thursday	*štvrtok*	weekend	*víkend*

Months
In Czech the months are very poetic and bear no resemblance to English. Slovak months are easier to recognise.

Words and phrases

January	*janu003 r*	July	*júl*
February	*február*	August	*august*
March	*marec*	September	*september*
April	*apríl*	October	*október*
May	*máj*	November	*november*
June	*jún*	December	*december*

Time

Yesterday/today/tomorrow	*Včera/dnes/zajtra*
Day/week/month/year	*Deň/týždeň/mesiac/rok*
Now/early/late	*Teraz/skoro/neskoro*

Basics

At your service (shops)	*Nech sa páči*
Excuse me (I'm sorry)	*Prepáčte*
Excuse me (Pardon?)	*Prosím?*
Good day	*Dobrý deň*
Good morning	*Dobré ráno*
Good night	*Dobrú noc*
Goodbye (familiar)	*Čau, ahoj*
Goodbye (polite)	*Dovidenia (adieu – zbohom)*
Hello (familiar)	*ahoj, čau, servus*

Language

Not at all!	*Niet za čo!*
Please	*Prosím*
Thank you	*Ďakujem Vám (Ti)*
Yes/no	*Áno/nie*

Meeting people

Do you speak English?	*Hovoríte po anglicky?*
Help!	*Pomoc!*
How are you?	*Ako sa máte? (máš)?*
I don't understand (Slovak)	*Nerozumiem (po slovensky)*
My name is …	*Volám sa …*
Pleased to meet you	*Teši ma*
Welcome!	*Vitajte!*
What's your name?	*Ako sa voláte?*

Questions

Can I help you?	*Môžem Vám pomôcť?*
Could you help me?	*Mohli by ste mi pomôcť?*
How far is it to …?	*Ako ďaleko je do… ?*
How much is it?	*Koľko to stojí?*
What?	*Čo?*
What does … mean?	*Čo znamená … ?*

Words and phrases

What is the fare?	*Koľko stojí lístok?*
What is the time?	*Koľko je hodín?*
When is …?	*Kedy je …?*
Where is …?	*Kde je …?*
Which bus goes to …?	*Ktorý autobus ide do …. ?*

Transport/travel

airport	*letisko*	platform/direction	*naštupište/smer*
arrivals/departure	*príchod/odchod*	return (ticket)	*tam a späť*
bicycle	*bicykel*	seat reservation	*miestenka*
border check	*hranicná kontrola*	ticket(s)	*lístok (lístky)*
bus (station)	*autobusová stanica*	timetable	*cestovný poriadok*
bus stop	*zastávka*	toilet	*WC/záchod*
customs	*colnica*	tram	*electrička*
ladies/gents	*ženi/muži*	trolleybus	*trolejbus*
main (railway)	*hlavná (železničná)*		
station, train	*stanica, vlak*		

Places

bridge	*most*	castle	*zámok*
castle		cemetery	*cintorín*
(fortress, ruins)	*hrad*	chateau, palace	*palác*

church	*kostol*	mountain	*hora*
embankment	*nábrežie*	park	*sad*
forest	*les*	river	*rieka*
garden	*záhrada*	road	*cesta*
gate	*brána*	square	*námestie*
highway	*diaľnica*	street	*ulica*
island	*ostrov*	town	*mesto*
lake	*jazero*	village	*dedina*

Hotel

Do you have any vacancies?	*Máte voľné izby?*
I would like a double room	*Chcem dvojposteľovú izbu*
first floor	*poschodie*
ground floor	*prízemie*
key	*kľúč*
room	*izba*
shower/bath	*sprcha*

In town

bank	*banka*	exhibition	*výstava*
bookshop	*kníhkupectvo*	hospital/doctor	*nemocnica/lekárov*
bureau de change	*zmenáreň*	market	*tržnica*
chemist	*lekáreň*	monument	*pamiatka*
consulate	*konzulát*	police	*policia*
embassy	*velvyslanectvo*	theatre	*divadlo*

Words and phrases

Post

airmail	*trieda*	Canada	*Kanada*
letter	*list*	England	*Anglicko, Veľká Británia*
post office	*pošta*	Hungary	*Maďarsko*
postcard	*pohľadnica*	Ireland	*Írsko*
stamps	*známka*	New Zealand	*Nový Zéland*
Australia	*Austrália*	USA	*Spojené štáty*
Austria	*Rakúsko*		*americké USA*

Eating and drinking

Another beer, please	*Ešte jedno pivo, prosím*
Bon appetite	*Dobrú chuť*
Cheers! Your health	*Na zdravie!*
Could I see the menu?	*Prosím si, menu/jedálny lístok?*
Do you have a table for 1, 2, 3?	*Máte stôl pre jedného, dvoch, troch?*
May I pay with a credit card?	*Môžem platiť kreditnou kartou?*
The bill, please	*Učet, prosím/Zaplatím*
Two beers, please	*Dvakrát pivo, prosím*
apple	*jablko*	beef	*hovädzie*
apricot	*marhuľa*	beer	*pivo*
bacon	*slanina*	beer hall	*piváreň*
baked	*zapečená*	boiled	*varený*

bread	*chlieb*	garlic	*cesnak*
breakfast	*raňajky*	a glass/bottle	*jeden pohár/fľaša*
butter	*maslo*	grapes	*hrozno*
cabbage	*kapusta*	green pepper	*paprika*
café	*kaviareň, cukáreň*	grilled	*grilovaný*
carp	*kapor*	ham	*šunka*
cheese	*syr*	ice cream	*zrmzlina*
chicken	*kuracie*	jam	*džem*
coffee	*káva*	juniper spirit (local)	*Borovička*
deep-fried giant		light/dark beer	*svetlé/tmavé pivo*
doughnut	*langoše*	lunch	*obed*
dinner	*večera*	meat	*mäso*
dry/sweet	*suché/sladké*	menu	*jedálny lístok*
duck	*kačica*	milk	*mlieko*
eggs	*vajíčka*	mushrooms	*huby, šampiňóny*
fish	*ryba*	mustard	*horčica*
frankfurters	*párky*	onion	*cibuľa*
fresh	*čerstvý*	orange	*pomaranč*
fried	*vyprážaný*	pancakes	*palacinky*
fruit and		peach	*broskyňa*
vegetables	*ovocie zelenina*	pear	*hruška*
game	*divina*	pies	*buchty*

Words and phrases

pork	*bravčové*	soup	*polievka*
poultry	*hydina*	stuffed	*plnený*
potato pancake	*lokša*	sugar	*cukor*
potatoes/chips	*zemiaky/hranolky*	take-away	*vziať si so sebou*
restaurant/canteen	*reštaurácia/jedáleň*	tap/mineral water	*čistá/minerálna voda*
rice	*ryža*	tea (with milk/	*čaj s mliekom/*
roasted	*opekaný*	with lemon)	*s citrónom*
salad	*šalát*	tomato	*paradajka, rajčina*
salmon	*losos*	trout	*pstruh*
salt/pepper	*soľ/korenie*	turkey	*morčacie*
sausages	*klobásy*	vegetarian dishes	*vegetariánske jedlo*
seafood	*morské jedlo*	white/red/rosé	*biele/červené/ružové*
sheep's cheese	*bryndza*	wine	*vino*
side dishes	*prílohy*	wine bar	*vináreň*
soft curd cheese	*tvaroh*		

Useful

cheap/expensive	*lacný/drahý*
east/west	*východ/západ*
entrance/exit	*vchod/východ*
good/bad	*dobrý/zlý*
hot/cold	*horúci/studený*

large/small	*veľký/malý*
lavatory	*záchod/WC (vay-tsay)*
left/right	*naľavo/napravo*
no smoking	*zákaz fajčiť*
north/south	*sever/juh*
old/new	*starý/nový*
open/closed (shops)	*otvorený/zatvorený*
push/pull (on doors)	*tam/sem*
red/yellow/green	*červeny/žltý/zelený*
white/black/blue	*biely/čierny/modrý*

13 Further information

BOOKS

History and culture

Brock, Peter *The Slovak National Awakening* University of Toronto Press, 1976

Chapman, Colin *August 21st. The Rape of Czechoslovakia* Cassell, 1968

Fonseca, Isabel *Bury Me Standing* Vintage, 1996

Henderson, Karen *Slovakia: The Escape from Invisibility* Routledge, 2002

Kirschbaum, Stanislav J *A History of Slovakia: The Struggle for Survival* 1996

Musil, Jirí (editor) *The End of Czechoslovakia* Central European UP, 1995

Petro, Peter *A History of Slovak Literature* Liverpool UP, 1996

Shawcross, William *Dubček and Czechoslovakia* Touchstone Books, 1990

Literature

Dobšinský, Pavol, adapted by Ann Macleod *The Enchanted Castle, and Other Tales and Legends* (1880–83) Hamlyn, 1967

Fermor, Patrick Leigh *A Time of Gifts* John Murray, 2004. Fermor's evocative walking journey from the Hook of Holland to the Middle Danube en route to Constantinople.

Hviezdoslav, Pavol Országh, translated by Jaroslav Vajda *Bloody Sonnets* Obrana Press, Scranton, PA, USA, 1950

Jašík, Rudolf, translated by Karol Kornel *Dead Soldiers Don't Sing* Artia, Prague, 1963

Kráľ, Janko, translated by Jaroslav Vajda *Janko Kráľ 1822–1972* Tatran, Bratislava, 1972

Kramoris, Ivan J *Anthology of Slovak Poetry* Obrana Press, Scranton, PA, USA, 1947

Mikszáth, Kálmán, translated by Dick Sturgess *The Siege of Beszterce* (1894). Corvina, Budapest, 1982. Hungarian novelist who set many of his stories in Slovakia.

Naughton, James (editor) *Eastern & Central Europe, Traveller's Literary Companion* In Print Publishing, 1995

Pynsent, Robert B (editor). *Modern Slovak Prose: Fiction since 1954* Macmillan, 1990

Šimečka, Martin M, translated by Peter Petro *The Year of the Frog (1985–90)* Louisiana State University Press, Baton Rouge, LA, and London, 1993. Mostly autobiographical account of young Slovak intellectual, whose father is a well-known dissident, living in Bratislava during the last years of communism.

Šmatlák, Stanislav, translated by M Hunningenová *Hviezdoslav: A National and World Poet* Obzor-Tatrapress, Bratislava, 1969

Sommer-Lefkovits, Elizabeth *Are You in this Hell Too?* Menard Press/Central Books, 1995. Harrowing Holocaust experience told by Slovak Jewish woman.

Guidebooks and maps

Freytag & Berndt *Automapa Slovenská republika* (1:250 000) www.freytagberndt.com

Barta, Vladimir *Hrady, Burgen, Castles* Ab Art Press, Bratislava, 1994

Lazistan, Eugen *Slovakia: A Photographic Odyssey* Neografia Martin, Slovakia 2001 (e vydavatelstvo@neografia.sk; www.neografia.sk)

Books

Kallay, Karol *Slovensko-Slowakei-Slovakia* Divided into four chapters with information on nature, architecture, culture and sports. Versions available in Slovak, German or English. Slovart Ltd, Bratislava, 1993

Lorinc, Sylvia & John M *Slovak–English–Slovak Dictionary and Phrasebook* Hippocrene Books, 1999

WEBSITES

www.bjs.sk Online edition of *Business Journal Slovakia*

www.bkis.sk Useful information at the BKIS Bratislava Cultural and Information Centre

www.bratislava.sk Bratislava City Hall's site is an excellent introduction to the city

www.bratislavahotels.com A directory and booking site for hotels

www.bratislavastags.com Local stag party organiser, run by Slovakia Green Tours

www.businessslovakia.com Latest news from World News network

www.cometoslovakia.com Slovakia for American travellers

www.dpb.sk Bratislava public transport

www.enjoyslovakia.com Hotels, city breaks, tourist information

www.feminet.sk Website for the feminist group in Bratislava

www.gay.sk Latest information on Bratislava's gay scene

www.greenpages.sk Online version of the *Slovak Spectator*'s *Book of Lists*

www.heartofeurope.co.uk Good introduction to Slovakia
www.imhd.sk Public transport in Bratislava explained clearly
www.kamdomesta.sk Online edition of the listings monthly *Kam do Mesta*
www.modra.sk Website for the wine-producing town of Modra
www.panorama.sk Slovakia document store
www.pezinok.sk Website for the wine-producing town of Pezinok
www.slovakiagreentours.com Good tour guide, also do stag parties
www.slovakspectator.sk Online edition of the *Slovak Spectator*, registration required
www.slovensko.com Good source for Slovak news, well presented, informative
www.stagbratislava.com Local stag party organisers
www.teos.sk Good English–Slovak–English dictionary
www.whatsonslovakia.com Online *Business Journal*'s entertainment magazine
www.zsr.sk Railways of Slovakia, timetables and information

WIN £100 CASH!

READER QUESTIONNAIRE

Send in your completed questionnaire for the chance to win
£100 cash in our regular draw
All respondents may order a Bradt guide at half the UK retail price – please
complete the order form overleaf.

Have you used any other Bradt guides? If so, which titles? ....

....

What other publishers' travel guides do you use regularly? ....

....

....

Where did you buy this guidebook? ....

What was the main purpose of your trip to Bratislava (or for what other reason did
you read our guide)? eg: holiday/business/charity etc. ....

....

What other destinations would you like to see covered by a Bradt guide?

....

What other destinations would you like to see covered by a Bradt guide?

. . . .

Would you like to receive our catalogue/newsletters?

YES / NO (If yes, please complete details on reverse)

If yes – by post or email?. . . . .

Age (circle relevant category) 16–25   26–45   46–60   60+

Male/Female (delete as appropriate)

Home country . . . .

Please send us any comments about our guide to Bratislava or other Bradt Travel Guides. . . . .

. . . .

. . . .

. . . .

Bradt Travel Guides

23 High Street, Chalfont St Peter, Bucks SL9 9QE, UK
Telephone: +44 1753 893444 Fax: +44 1753 892333
Email: info@bradtguides.com
www.bradtguides.com

CLAIM YOUR HALF-PRICE BRADT GUIDE!

To order your half-price copy of a Bradt guide, and to enter our £100 prize draw, fill in the form below, complete the questionnaire on pages 248–9, and send it to us by post, fax or email. Details of some Bradt city guides can be found on pages XII–XIII; the full range of titles and prices is on our website (www.bradtguides.com).

Title	Retail price	Half price
. . . .	. . . .	. . . .
Post & packing (£1/book UK; £2/book Europe; £3/book rest of world)		. . . .
	Total	. . . .

Name . . . .
. . . .
Address. . . . .
. . . .
Tel . . . . Email . . . .

❏ I enclose a cheque for £ . . . . made payable to Bradt Travel Guides Ltd
❏ I would like to pay by VISA or MasterCard
    Number . . . . Expiry date . . . .
❏ Please add my name to your catalogue mailing list.

Index

252

Blue Church of St Elizabeth (AAS)

Bratislava Castle, the 'upside-down bedstead' (AAS)

Sculpture of man in manhole, on Panská (J)

Michael's Tower (AAS)

Nový most bridge and the UFO café (JB)

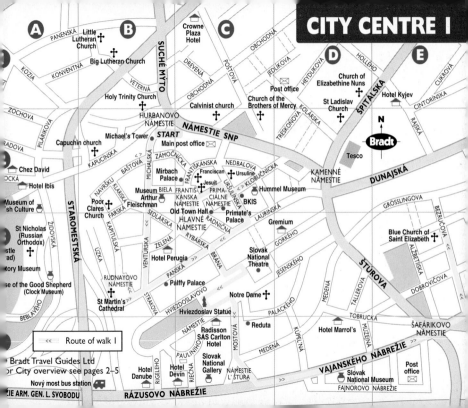

CITY CENTRE I

PANENSKÁ · Little Lutheran Church · Big Lutheran Church · KONVENTNÁ · KOZIA · SUCHÉ MÝTO · DREVENÁ · OBCHODNÁ · Crowne Plaza Hotel · POŠTOVÁ · JEDLÍKOVA · HEYDUKOVA · HOLLÉHO · Church of Elizabethine Nuns · SPITÁLSKA · CUKROVÁ · Hotel Kyjev · CINTORÍNSKA · RAJSKÁ

VETERNÁ · Holy Trinity Church · HURBANOVO NÁMESTIE · Calvinist church · Church of the Brothers of Mercy · St Ladislav Church · KOLÁRSKA · TRESKOŇOVA

ZOCHOVA · PILÁRIKOVA · RADOVA · Capuchin church · NÁMESTIE SNP · KAMENNÉ NÁMESTIE · Tesco · **Bradt** · N · DUNAJSKÁ

Michael's Tower · START · Main post office · ZÁMOČNÍCKA · MICHALSKÁ · BAŠTOVÁ · FRANTIŠKÁNSKA · NEDBALOVA · Ursuline · KLOBUČNÍCKA · Hummel Museum · GROSSLINGOVA · BEZRUČOVA

Chez David · Hotel Ibis · Museum of ...sh Culture · NAVRSKU · KLARISKÁ · Mirbach Palace · BIELA · FRANTIŠ-KÁNSKE NÁMESTIE · Jesuit · CIALNE NÁMESTIE · PRIMA-... · URŠULÍNSKA · BKIS · Museum Arthur Fleischman · Poor Clares Church · FARSKÁ · KAPITULSKÁ · Old Town Hall · HLAVNÉ NÁMESTIE · RADNIČNÁ · Primate's Palace · LAURINSKÁ · Gremium · GORKÉHO · Blue Church of Saint Elizabeth · ALŽBETINA

St Nicholas (Russian Orthodox) · ...stle ...ad) · ...tory Museum · ...se of the Good Shepherd (Clock Museum) · STAROMESTSKÁ · UZKÁ · SEDLÁRSKA · VENTÚRSKA · ZELENÁ · RYBÁRSKA · BRÁNA · Hotel Perugia · PANSKÁ · Slovak National Theatre · JESENSKÉHO · ŠTÚROVA · DOBROVIČOVA

RUDNAYOVO NÁMESTIE · St Martin's Cathedral · STRAKOVA · Pálffy Palace · HVIEZDOSLAVOVO · Notre Dame · Hviezdoslav Statue · NÁMESTIE · Reduta · PALACKÉHO · MEDENA · Hotel Marrol's · TOBRUCKÁ · TALLEROVA · MÚZEJNÁ · KUPELNÁ · ŠAFÁRIKOVO NÁMESTIE

Radisson SAS Carlton Hotel · MOSTOVÁ · Slovak National Gallery · Slovak National Museum · VAJANSKÉHO NÁBREŽIE · Post office

☐☐☐ Route of walk 1

Hotel Danube · Hotel Devín · RIGEĽÉHO · PAULINÍHO · RIEČNA · NÁMESTIE Ľ. ŠTÚRA · FAJNOROVO NÁBREŽIE

...Bradt Travel Guides Ltd
...or City overview see pages 2–5
Nový most bus station

...IE ARM. GEN. L. SVOBODU · RÁZUSOVO NÁBREŽIE

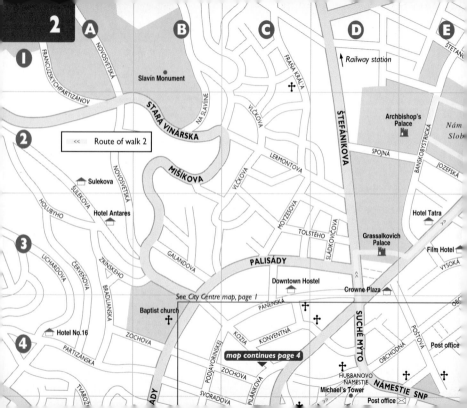

2

A

I

FRANCÚZSKYCH PARTIZÁNOV
NOVOSVETSKÁ

Slavín Monument

STARÁ VINÁRSKA

2

<<< Route of walk 2

NOVOSVETSKÁ
ŠULEKOVA
HOLUBYHO

Sulekova

MIŠÍKOVA

Hotel Antares

3

LICHARDOVA
ČERVENOVA
BRADLIANSKA
ZRÍNSKEHO

GALANDOVA

Baptist church

4

Hotel No.16

PARTIZÁNSKA
TVAROŽ

ZOCHOVA

ADY

B

NA SLAVÍNE

C

FRAŇA KRÁĽA

VLČKOVA

LERMONTOVA

VLČKOVA

MOYZESOVA

TOLSTÉHO

PALISÁDY

See City Centre map, page 1

Downtown Hostel

PANENSKÁ

KOZIA
KONVENTNÁ

map continues page 4

PODJAVORINSKEJ
ZOCHOVA
PILÁRIKOVA
SVORADOVA

D

↑ Railway station

ŠTEFÁNIKOVA

SPOJNÁ

SLADKOVIČOVA

Grassalkovich
Palace

Crowne Plaza

SUCHÉ MÝTO

OBCHODNÁ

HURBANOVO
NÁMESTIE

Michael's Tower

NÁMESTIE SNP

Post office ✉

E

ŠTEFÁN

Archbishop's
Palace

BANSKOBYSTRICKÁ

Nám
Slob

JOZEFSKÁ

Hotel Tatra

Film Hotel

VYSOKÁ

ORC

POŠTOVÁ

Post office

Post office

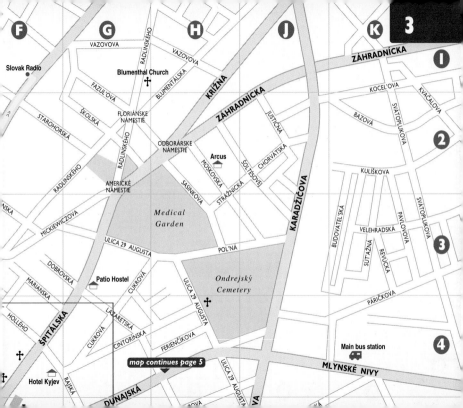

map continues page 5

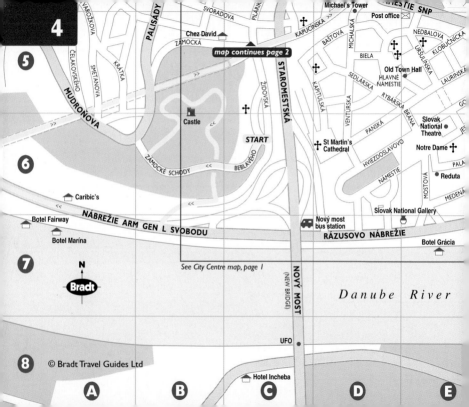

4

5

6

7

8

VAROŽKOVA

CELAKOVSKEHO

MUDROŇOVA

SMETANOVA

KRATKA

PALISÁDY

SVORADOVA

PILARIK

ZÁMOCKÁ

Chez David

map continues page 2

ZÁMOCKÉ SCHODY

ŽIDOVSKA

STAROMESTSKÁ

Castle

START

BEBLAVÉHO

Caribic's

NÁBREŽIE ARM GEN L SVOBODU

Botel Fairway

Botel Marína

See City Centre map, page 1

N

Bradt

© Bradt Travel Guides Ltd

Michael's Tower

Post office ✉

MESTIE SNP

KAPUCÍNSKA

MICHALSKA

NEDBALOVA

BÁSTOVA

BIELA

URŠULINSKÁ

KLOBUČNÍCKA

Old Town Hall

SEDLARSKA

HLAVNÉ NAMESTIE

LAURINSKA

KAPITULSKA

RYBÁRSKA BRÁNA

VENTURSKA

PANSKA

Slovak National Theatre

GO

JES

St Martin's Cathedral

HVIEZDOSLAVOVO

Notre Dame ✝

NAMESTIE

MOSTOVA

PALA

Reduta

MEDENA

Slovak National Gallery

Nový most bus station

RÁZUSOVO NÁBREŽIE

Botel Grácia

NOVÝ MOST (NEW BRIDGE)

Danube River

UFO

Hotel Incheba

A　　**B**　　**C**　　**D**　　**E**

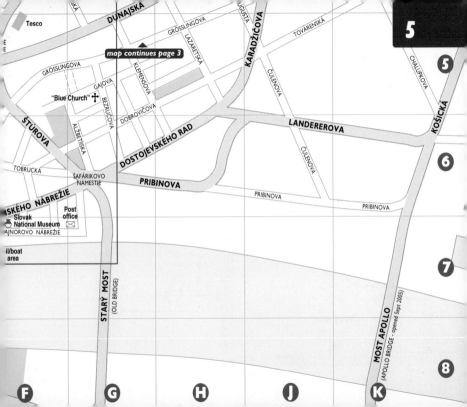

Tesco

DUNAJSKÁ

GRÖSSLINGOVA

KARADŽIČOVA

AUGUSTA

TOVÁRENSKÁ

CHALÚPKOVA

map continues page 3

GRÖSSLINGOVA

LAZARETSKÁ

KLEMENSOVA

GAJOVA

"Blue Church" ✝

BEZRUČOVA

DOBROVIČOVA

ČULENOVA

LANDEREROVA

KOŠICKÁ

ŠTÚROVA

ALŽBETIISKA

DOSTOJEVSKÉHO RAD

6

TOBRUCKÁ

ČULENOVA

ŠAFÁRIKOVO NÁMESTIE

PRIBINOVA

...SKÉHO NÁBREŽIE

PRIBINOVA

PRIBINOVA

Post office

Slovak National Museum 🏛 ✉

...AJNOROVO NÁBREŽIE

...il/boat area

7

STARÝ MOST

(OLD BRIDGE)

MOST APOLLO

(APOLLO BRIDGE) - opened Sept 2005)

8

F

G

H

J

K

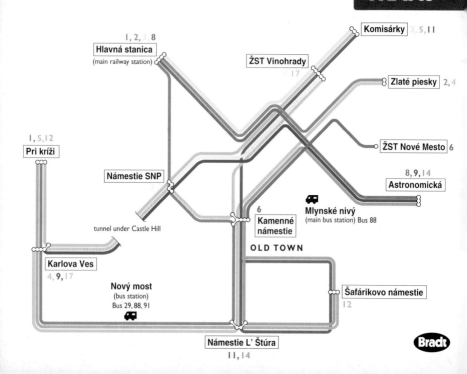

TRAMS

Komisárky 3, 5, 11

1, 2, 3, 8
Hlavná stanica
(main railway station)

ŽST Vinohrady
17

Zlaté piesky 2, 4

ŽST Nové Mesto 6

1, 5, 12
Pri kríži

Námestie SNP

8, 9, 14
Astronomická

6
Kamenné námestie

Mlynské nivy
(main bus station) Bus 88

tunnel under Castle Hill

Karlova Ves
4, 9, 17

OLD TOWN

Nový most
(bus station)
Bus 29, 88, 91

Šafárikovo námestie
12

Námestie Ľ' Štúra
11, 14

Bradt